Work Sm Not Harder

Work Smarter, Not Harder has been used as the basis for our internal training for both our Sales Team, and Operation and Administration Support. It provides easy-to-follow steps to demonstrate that your destiny is of your own making.

GORDON ATKINS, NATIONAL MANAGER, FINANCIAL MARKETING SERVICES, TOYOTA AUSTRALIA

Work Smarter, Not Harder is a book that is required reading for all who aim to achieve their full potential. You will enjoy every chapter.

DOUG NETTLESHIP, EDITOR, BUSINESS BULLETIN

I have trained my middle management team to work smarter, not harder by supplying each of them with a copy of this book and then working through it with them over a four-week period. I have now bought around 40 copies of the book and have recommended it to many other people.

BARRY GORDON, MARKETING MANAGER, QUEST NEWSPAPERS

Throughout my business career I have read many books on selling, motivation and time study, most of which have been written by celebrated international 'experts'; but I can say in all honesty that I have gained far more from this book than all others put together.

PETER ALLEN, MANAGING DIRECTOR, IMAGE SPORTS

Work Smarter, Not Harder is a success manual of powerful techniques and strategies that will enhance personal productivity and effectiveness. This book is invaluable because it will help you position yourself for success in rapidly changing and competitive times.

CHRISTINE SILINK, FOUNDER & PRESIDENT, DYNAMIS CLUB

Work Smarter, Not Harder is one of the best books I have read for time management tips and for motivating me to set my business and personal goals, down on paper for the first time in my life.

HELEN COOK, COOK & ASSOCIATES, VICTORIA

Work
Smarter
Not
Harder

Work Smarter Not Harder

JACK COLLIS
AND MICHAEL LEBOEUF

HarperBusiness
An imprint of HarperCollins*Publishers*

Acknowledgements

With grateful thanks to all those who have supported and endorsed WORK SMARTER, NOT HARDER. Special thanks to the HarperBusiness team.

Harper*Business*
An imprint of HarperCollins*Publishers,* Australia

First published in Australia in 1988 by Goal Getting Seminars
This Harper*Business* edition published in 1995
Reprinted 1996 (twice), 1998, 1999, 2000 (twice), 2001 (twice), 2002, 2003
by HarperCollins*Publishers* Pty Limited
ABN 36 009 913 517
A member of the HarperCollins*Publishers* (Australia) Pty Limited Group
www.harpercollins.com.au

HarperCollins*Publishers*
25 Ryde Road, Pymble, Sydney, NSW 2073, Australia
31 View Road, Glenfield, Auckland 10, New Zealand
77-85 Fulham Palace Road, London W6 8JB, United Kingdom
Hazelton Lanes, 55 Avenue Road, Suite 2900, Toronto, Ontario M5R 3L2
and 1995 Markham Road, Scarborough, Ontario M1B 5M8, Canada
10 East 53rd Street, New York NY 10022, USA

National Library of Australia Cataloguing-in-Publication data:

Collis, Jack.
    Work smarter, not harder.
    ISBN 0 7322 5617 8.
    1. Conduct of life. 2. Success. 3. Achievement motivation.
    I. LeBoeuf, Michael. II. Title.
158.1

Set in Goudy 10/12
Printed and bound in Australia by Griffin Press on 79gsm Bulky Paperback White

14 13 12 11   03 04 05 06

Jack Collis

Jack Collis has been helping others to work smarter and more effectively for most of his working life. A former International Marketing Manager for AMP, he is now a successful speaker, author and business consultant.

Jack Collis has written numerous books including *Yes You Can*, *Your Business and Your Customer* and *Work Smarter, Not Harder* with Michael LeBoeuf. Jack is a recognised leader in the fields of personal development, mindpower, motivation and creative marketing. He has also developed and published specialised training programs for leading organisations. Jack is a prize winning and prolific artist. He is a wonderful example of the power of working smarter, not harder.

Michael LeBoeuf

Michael LeBoeuf's mission is to help people find solid, practical ways to live and work smarter. An international author, business consultant and speaker, Dr LeBoeuf taught management organisational behaviour and communication at the University of New Orleans for 20 years.

His books include *Imagineering*, *How to Win Customers and Keep them for Life*, *How to Win a Lot More Business in a Lot Less Time* and *Work Smarter, Not Harder* with Jack Collis. His books have been translated and published in as many as ten languages and adapted to produce 12 different audio and video programs.

CONTENTS

INTRODUCTION

*In order that people may be happy in their work,
these three things are needed: They must be
fit for it. They must not do too much of it.
And they must have a sense of success in it.*

JOHN RUSKIN

WORK SMARTER, NOT HARDER is about unlocking our
real potential. It is about how to simplify our life and increase our
chances of achieving those goals that are important to us. It is about
the belief that each of us has the power to create the life we want if we
have the self-discipline to unlock our potential. It is about enjoying
each day because we are in control of our own lives. It is about focusing on priorities and understanding that life really is a self-fulfilling
prophecy in that our actions create our future.

Work Smarter, Not Harder is not about saving a few minutes each
hour, or a day each week. It is not about becoming a time-and-motion
expert. It doesn't encourage clock watching as a pursuit in itself. It is not
about being busy, because often we can best use our time by stopping
work and starting to think. We need to examine what we are doing to
ensure that it is taking us in the right direction. If we have no direction,
what we do is not important. Going nowhere requires no special skill.

This book doesn't outline a system that you must follow from start to
finish. The issue of personal productivity is too complex for a one-
system approach. What may be helpful to one person may be useless to
another. You have to choose what is important to you at any given time.
Work Smarter, Not Harder is about giving you worthwhile choices. It is
filled with practical, results-oriented methods, techniques and tactics

that work and are working today for thousands of people who have listened to our cassettes, attended our seminars or read our articles on using time effectively, goal achieving and personal motivation.

Most of us want to know how to get the greatest return on our investment of time and energy. In other words, how to get more done while spending less time and energy.

Through experience and research, both Michael and I, have found the following to be the major contributors to failure and fatigue:

◆ An unwillingness to invest in work today for the rewards it will produce in the future.

◆ Many people make only a halfhearted effort and then abandon their goals.

◆ Having programmed, erroneous beliefs that we have all been taught about work.

◆ Not knowing or deciding what you want out of life.

◆ Poor time management.

◆ A weak self-image, fear of failure, guilt, worry, excessive anger, and other irrational time- and energy-draining emotions.

◆ Procrastination.

◆ The unwillingness or inability to skilfully delegate tasks to others.

◆ Communication breakdowns.

◆ Unnecessary interpersonal conflicts.

◆ Common interruptions, such as meetings, visitors and telephone calls.

◆ A deluge of paperwork.

This book outlines the causes of and cures for each of these factors in a simple, readable and practical format to make it immediately useful.

If you buy this book, read it, put it on the shelf and forget it, you won't get your money's worth. However, if you follow the recommendations given, this book can represent the beginning of a rewarding growth experience.

First, be an active reader. Read with a pencil or pen in your hand. When you come across a key idea that applies to you, underline it or make notes in the margin. After reading each chapter, make a list of concepts and worksavers that apply to you and resolve to use them.

Second, don't attempt to make wholesale, abrupt changes in your behaviour. The best and most effective way to implement change is gradually, smoothly and systematically. As you compile a list of worksaving ideas, resolve to apply one new idea each week. That may sound like slow progress, but if you do that you will have put over 50 new effectiveness techniques into your life in one year. If you prefer, try out two or three new ideas a week, but back off if you begin to feel uncomfortable.

Don't expect to be perfect. There will be days when you will not or cannot do the things you feel you should or could have done. Some days, you simply may not give a damn. Other days, Murphy's Law may rear its ugly head. (Read about Murphy's Law, and what to do about it, in Chapter 1.) Just resolve to keep trying. Improving your effectiveness is like playing golf. Theoretically, the perfect golf score is 18, but to achieve that you would have to score a hole in one on 18 consecutive holes. Obviously, no one will ever achieve the perfect score. But this doesn't stop millions of avid duffers from trying to improve their score each week. As you strive to work smarter, take a similar approach. Resolve to improve, but realise that a perfect result is not always possible.

The changes currently taking place in our working environment are changing our world forever. They are massive and constant, and the future promises no respite. Technology is driving the change in a relentless push that cannot be stopped. The swifter communications become, the more relentless the change. All of this activity is producing new opportunities for each of us if we can but see them. The challenge for each of us is to see with new eyes, to perceive with new wisdom, and to act with speed and purpose to claim our share of these new and exciting times.

Parts 1 to 4 of this book will equip you with the habits and skills that will enable you to stake your claim with confidence. Part 5, 'Looking Ahead', deals with the major changes that are starting to shape our careers and our lives and which will dominate the work place in the future. The suggestions contained in this part of the book will ensure that you get your share of the opportunities the future holds.

JACK COLLIS

PART 1

THE
EFFECTIVENESS
PLAN

CHAPTER 1

WORKAHOLICS UNANIMOUS

When work is a pleasure, life is a joy!
When work is a duty, life is slavery.
MAXIM GORKY

TIME EQUALS MONEY. How often have we heard this statement? Yet the reality of life for the great majority of us is that work equals money. If you think time equals money, stop work and see how much money you make. A man or woman at work, or a dollar at work, is the reality of making money. If you are not working and have no dollars at work for you, you won't be making money but you will still be using up your quota of time.

Time equals money only if it is accepted that the quality of your work decides the value of your time. Work is the lot of humanity. For some it is the very fibre of their life — enjoyable, productive and rewarding. For others it is a drudgery, and something to be endured.

What does work mean to you? Do you think of it as an activity that takes more from you than it returns? Do you think of the distinction between play and work as that between pleasure and pain? Do you live to work? Do you work to live? Regardless of your answers, one thing is certain: work is here to stay. By work, I mean the expenditure of time and energy (both physical and mental) to complete a task. This definition is a very broad one. When you stop and think about it, it means that you spend the overwhelming majority of your waking hours at work. When you brush your teeth, plan a holiday, drive to work, or perform household or occupational chores, you are at work. Similarly, you may work at being a better doctor, lawyer, teacher, tennis player, lover or cook. Work, like death and taxes, is an all-encompassing and inescapable fact of life.

Now for the good news. In this book, you will find many simple but powerful ideas and techniques that will enable you to conquer your personal energy crisis.

Do you ever feel frustrated and exhausted at the end of the day because you have nothing to show for your efforts? I'll show you some simple techniques that will make every day count and leave you with time and energy to spare.

Do you find yourself rushing to meet deadlines and being hassled by an unending stream of crises? I'll describe some ways to beat the deadline hassle and cut down on your firefighting activities.

Is your life one big mass of commitments that leave you feeling confused and immobilised? I'll show you how to organise those commitments, eliminate many and give yourself a sense of direction.

Do you feel guilty about what doesn't get done and worried about what may not get done? I'll convince you that these are useless emotions that only cause you to work more and accomplish less.

Do you find yourself not tackling important projects because they seem overwhelming or unpleasant? I'll explain how you can gain momentum to tackle these projects and follow through to successful completion.

Are you compulsive about having to do everything yourself? I'll give you some tips on successful delegating.

In working with others, do you often find the going is rough due to communication breakdowns and unnecessary conflicts? I'll point out some common pitfalls of communication and conflict, and recommend ways of avoiding them.

Do you find that your work is hampered by interruptions such as meetings, visitors and telephone calls? I'll give you some pointers for minimising them.

Are you drowning in a sea of information and paper overload, as most of us are? I'll show you how to quieten down the paper tiger to a mild roar.

I am confident that you will be able to benefit from many, if not all, of the ideas contained in this book. And the best part is that they are simple, proven and immediately applicable.

EFFECTIVENESS — THE KEY TO IT ALL

As you read this, you may be thinking that this is a book written by an efficiency nut who wants to turn you into an unfeeling, unthinking automaton. Nothing could be further from the truth.

All too often, many of us confuse effectiveness with efficiency. Being effective entails choosing the right goals from a set of alternatives and then achieving them. Efficiency, on the other hand, assumes that the goals are self-evident and then proceeds to find the best means of achieving them. Efficiency is doing the job right, whereas effectiveness is doing the right job. In a nutshell, effectiveness means results. Both are valuable concepts but, to my mind, effectiveness is far more important.

TIME — YOUR MOST VALUABLE RESOURCE

What is your time worth? (See the table on the next page.) Benjamin Franklin, the American statesman and scientist, told us that time is money; and in the business sense, this is true. Time is like money in that it is measurable and you can't take it with you. However, as a resource, time has unique properties. We are forced to use time at a constant rate. The inventory is being depleted at an amount of 60 minutes an hour, 24 hours a day, 168 hours a week. Time is irreplaceable. We are all given a finite amount of time, but the irony is that we never know how much time we have until we run out of it. Few of us admit to having enough time, but all of us have all that there is; that is the paradox of time. Time is truly our most precious resource.

How old are you? How many more years do you expect to live? I ask these questions not to depress you, but rather to impress on you the briefness of our earthly existence. Waste your money and you're only out of money, but waste your time and you have lost a part of your life. Few of us would knowingly take half of our take-home pay and spend

WHAT IS YOUR TIME WORTH?

If you earn $	Every minute is worth $	Every hour is worth $	Over a year, one hour a day is worth $
2 000	0.0170	1.02	250
2 500	0.0213	1.28	312
3 000	0.0256	1.54	375
3 500	0.0300	1.79	437
4 000	0.0341	2.05	500
5 000	0.0426	2.56	625
6 000	0.0513	3.07	750
7 000	0.0598	3.59	875
10 000	0.0852	5.12	1 250
20 000	0.1708	10.25	2 500
25 000	0.2135	12.81	3 125
30 000	0.2561	15.37	3 750
35 000	0.2988	17.93	4 375
40 000	0.3415	20.49	5 000
50 000	0.4269	25.61	6 250
75 000	0.6403	38.42	9 375
100 000	0.8523	51.23	12 500

Based on 244 eight-hour working days.

it on something that was of absolutely no use to us or anyone else. However, the vast majority of us spend at least 50 per cent of each day on various pastimes that are of no use or satisfaction to anyone, including ourselves. We literally waste half our lives and do it in oblivious indifference.

So true.

Coming to grips with our mortality can either help us or hurt us. If we choose to let it hurt us, we can wallow in the futility and tragedy of life. We can conclude that life isn't worth living. Or, as most of us do, we can fool ourselves and believe that our time is infinite, that there will always be tomorrow to fulfil our lifetime dreams and wishes. Fortunately, some people deal with mortality in a more constructive way. In effect, these people say to themselves, 'I'm not going to be here forever, so I'd better make the most of every minute, hour, day and year.' They view life as a brief but wonderful experience to be enjoyed to the full. They live their lives for themselves because they accept that their life is all they have. They accept responsibility for their own feelings, triumphs and misfortunes. As a result of this take-charge attitude, these people realise the necessity to plan their lives for maximum personal satisfaction.

In order to make the most of your future time and energy, it is imperative that you devote some of your present time and energy to planning. Without sound plans to increase our personal effectiveness, we drift and stagnate. Some people believe that planning is merely deciding what to do *in* the future. However, a better definition of planning is deciding what you have to do in order to *have* a future.

THE INVESTMENT THEORY OF WORK

Simply put, the investment theory of work states that you must be willing to sacrifice some of your present time, energy and short-range satisfactions in order to work less and accomplish more later on.

There is nothing new or earth-shattering about the investment theory of work, and we have all used it from time to time. When you take on a part-time job in addition to your regular duties in order to save for a new house or car, or when you put time aside for additional or advanced training, you are applying the investment theory.

Most of us, however, don't rely on it systematically as a working principle in our lives. The reason for this is what I call the instant-everything lifestyle. This has become the prevailing attitude in our society. Pick up any newspaper, turn on the radio or television, or drive down any major city or country road, and voices from the land of instant everything will announce their readiness to satisfy your every need.

Are you hungry or thirsty? There are fast-food restaurants and express checkout supermarkets by the score. Do you dislike the way you look? There are literally thousands of establishments crying out to make you lighter, heavier, sexier, healthier or more beautiful. Do you want to change your mood? There are pills and potions to pick you up, bring you down, keep you awake and put you to sleep. The list is endless; it's the miracle of life in the 20th century.

One of the problems with instant everything is that it lulls us into neglecting the future. All that matters is the urgency of satisfying our present needs. However, the future is not instant. It runs on a very precise schedule and takes its time getting here. Tomorrow is promised to no one, but it is also a fact that most of us will be here when it arrives. Fail to control your future and it will control you. Your use of time and energy will be dictated by circumstances rather than by yourself. The relationship between you and time is always one of master and slave. There is no middle ground. The only question lies in which role you choose to play.

Many of the ideas suggested in this book will at first be unfamiliar and involve a greater initial investment of work than do the old, comfortable habits to which you have grown accustomed. However, as the Queen said to Alice in Lewis Carroll's *Through the Looking-Glass*, 'It's a poor sort of memory that only works backwards.' As your 'two-way memory' looks forward, you will realise that the rewards are greater accomplishments coupled with less expenditure of your time and energy.

I believe that happiness and success don't just happen to someone — they happen when opportunity meets preparation. Those who succeed do so because they were willing to invest in the groundwork and were prepared when the tide of good fortune rolled in.

Working smart requires an investment of thought, self-discipline and change. You must be willing to carefully examine and evaluate your present feelings, values, attitudes and work habits. Anyone who has ever been faced with the task of objective self-evaluation will agree that, while not pleasant, it was enlightening. Once you have completed your self-examination, you must be willing to change your thinking and behaviour to that which is more beneficial. Old habits die hard and change is tough, so you must discipline yourself until the new behaviour becomes old habit. The whole process is one of getting mentally tough with yourself in the short run to make it easier on yourself in the long run.

Caution: Program Error

We all have ideas, values, biases and theories about work. For the purposes of simplicity, let's refer to them as 'work tapes': recorded messages about work stored away in the recesses of our brain. Some of these tapes we are aware of, while others dwell at the subconscious level. Nevertheless, all of them program our behaviour from time to time. We acquire work tapes from sources such as parents, teachers, bosses, colleagues, experience, religion, the media and the government.

The problem is that in most situations, these tapes are at best incomplete truths and at worst, total fantasies. Yet many of us play them automatically and practise their prescriptions with dogmatic zeal. The result is more work coupled with little or no accomplishment and accompanying frustration.

Listed below are 12 widely believed, highly mythological work tapes. This list is by no means complete. As you read each of them, try to think of someone you know who lives and practises or has practised these injunctions. Is it you? If you are totally honest with yourself, you will probably see yourself in at least some of them.

1. 'THE MORE YOU SWEAT, THE MORE YOU GET' *ME !!*

Called by some 'the buckets of sweat syndrome', this myth would have you believe that results are directly related to how hard you work. An abundance of proverbs reinforce the concept of equating results with hard work. 'Keep your shoulder to the wheel and your nose to the grindstone'; 'The harder I work, the luckier I get'; and Thomas Edison's 'Genius is one percent inspiration and ninety-nine percent perspiration' are a few examples.

When asked the key to our success, the first thing we usually attribute it to is hard work. So ingrained in our thinking is the 'hard work' ethic that we instinctively lay claim to having this quality, as if it shows a weakness if we do not and a strength if we do. Many who claim to have succeeded largely through hard work conveniently ignore elements of influence which worked in their favour. As Don Marquis, the American satirist, said, 'When a man tells you he got rich through hard work, ask him, Whose?'

We hear a lot about hard work and success, but hard work and failure probably occurs just as often. Some of us work hard at our jobs and get fired. Others work hard at marriages that fail. Still others study hard and fail to get promoted, to graduate or to find a job.

Sometimes hard work does make the difference between success and failure. The problem is that we tend to overstate its value and ignore other equally important criteria for success. Fortunately, or unfortunately, results are seldom if ever proportional to the effort expended. Keeping your shoulder to the wheel and your nose to the grindstone only guarantees you two things: a warped posture and a flat nose.

2. 'ACTIVITY MEANS PRODUCTIVITY'

Many of us habitually confuse activity with results. This can be observed frequently on the job. Often, organisations find it hard to measure an employee's effectiveness. Consequently, activity replaces results as the yardstick of performance. The busiest beaver is deemed to be the best worker and is rewarded for busy behaviour rather than results.

The time clock is another great contributor to busy behaviour. Many of us have nine-to-five jobs and sometimes there are days when there is little or nothing to do. Still, in most cases, we are required to show up and stay the whole day, regardless of the workload. All that this does is create a breeding ground for time- and energy-wasting behaviour. After all, if you don't look busy, the boss may decide you are dispensable.

Ironically, we feel compelled to stay busy when we are least secure about what we should be doing. All too often we redouble our efforts after losing sight of our objectives. We try to fill a void of purpose with activity. This is expressed well by a saying in the French Foreign Legion: 'When in doubt, gallop!'

The activity trap is beaten by setting goals and keeping them in focus. Failure to keep goals in focus is where most of us go astray. In the process of pursuing a goal, it's easy to get lost in a myriad of activities. The unfortunate result is that these activities become the end, rather than a means to an end. It's the classic case of the tail wagging the dog. As the American poet and essayist Henry David Thoreau said, 'It's not enough to be busy . . . the question is: What are we busy about?'

3. 'EFFICIENCY MEANS EFFECTIVENESS'

The confusion that arises between efficiency and effectiveness was discussed earlier. The point I wish to make here is that effectiveness must precede efficiency. How can you find the best way to achieve a goal if you don't know what the goal is? The good news is that effectiveness can be learned. You can, by the wise use of goals and priorities, increase your productivity significantly.

4. 'Burn The Midnight Oil'

This myth fosters the belief that results are proportionate to the amount of time spent in pursuing a goal. Career workaholics are common victims of this myth. Seen at the office at night and on weekends, they allocate every possible moment to the job. Other things in life, such as sleep, family and diversions, are all placed in a distant second category of importance.

There are definite dangers involved in working long hours. First, we tend to get dull after expending a good amount of time on a task. We need to get away and recharge our batteries. Failure to do this hampers our enthusiasm and creativity. Second, if you acquire the long-hours habit, there is always tonight or this weekend to tackle writing that report or answering those letters. You allow Parkinson's Law into your life: work expands to fill the time available. Finally, the price that many of us pay for this type of behaviour is exorbitant. Nervous breakdowns, ill health, divorce, alcoholism and premature death are common among those who buy the midnight oil program.

5. 'The Best Way To Get The Job Done Is To Do It Yourself'

The argument for such a philosophy seems sound. You don't have to call or pay someone else to do the job and, by doing it yourself, you don't have to check up to ensure that the job was completed satisfactorily. It also saves the time involved in explaining to someone else what to do and how to do it.

There are times when doing it yourself is the answer. However, this is generally not the case, for two reasons. First, despite your feelings of omnipotence, you have limitations. You may immerse yourself in a project only to find that you don't have the time, training or tools necessary to successfully complete it. You may even complicate the problem, making the situation worse. Anyone who has ever tackled complicated household repairs and improvements has fallen into this trap. You run the risk of pouring your time and energy into a bottomless pit and with little to show for it.

The second and more important reason for avoiding the do-it-yourself attitude is that it dilutes your effectiveness. Devoting a little of yourself to everything means committing a great deal of yourself to nothing. This leaves you unable to concentrate on those very few projects that have the highest payoff per investment of your time and energy. Why scatter your efforts by using the shotgun approach when you can concentrate them and be a big gun?

⬤⬤ 6. 'THE EASY WAY IS THE BEST WAY'

When the great philosopher, Linus, said, 'No problem is so big or so complicated that it can't be run away from!' he was espousing the myth of taking the easy way out. Very often the 'easy way' tape is adopted by those who previously followed the 'hard work' tape. When all their work fails to bring the expected results, they become disenchanted. Instead of examining the situation logically and trying to learn from it, they simply remove one tape and plug in another.

Those who take the easy way out in life are not aware of, or choose to ignore, the investment theory of work. Unfortunately, they generally discover that the path of least resistance carries a hidden price tag. They never seem to learn one of life's greatest truths: life is difficult.

From birth to death, life is a process of solving problems. The greater our discipline, the greater our ability to solve life's problems. The more we solve our problems, the easier life becomes and the greater our chances of achieving goals that are important to us. Those who take the easy way out take a short-term patching approach to life, leaving tomorrow up for grabs. The reality is that nothing is easy. The path of least resistance is for losers.

⬤⬤ 7. 'HARD WORK IS VIRTUOUS'

One of the traditions of our society is that there is virtue and nobility in hard work. 'He's a hard worker' is considered a compliment. The idea that work is good in itself, and that people at work not only make a contribution to their fellows but become better people by virtue of the act of working, is so strongly held that many people cannot handle the feelings of guilt and unworthiness when they become unemployed, even to the extent of ending their lives. Among the values in our society, this one goes almost totally unchallenged.

To assume that any human activity carries with it 100 per cent inherent virtuousness is questionable. Hard work makes some people and breaks others. It depends on the person and the work in question.

▣ 8. 'Work Is Not Fun'

The explanation of work in the Old Testament paints a very bleak picture. Work is regarded as a punishment for sins, and people must spend most of their waking hours toiling away at backbreaking labour in order to survive. Thus, from the Book of Genesis another pervasive value was born: work is not to be enjoyed. Abraham Lincoln expressed the idea when he said, 'My father taught me to work, but not to love it. I never did like to work, and I don't deny it. I'd rather read, tell stories, crack jokes, talk, laugh, anything but work.'

Of all the programmed myths, we seem to be making our best progress towards deactivating this one. Most of us realise that the exertion of mental and physical energy is totally natural. Depending on the individual and the work, work can be most enjoyable, highly unpleasant or somewhere in-between. The trouble in following this tape is that if you believe there is only unpleasantness in work, then that is all you will perceive and you run a high risk of shortchanging yourself of some of life's greatest satisfactions.

▣ 9. 'There Is Only One Best Way'

Most of our formal education conditions us to think this way. At school and university, we spend most of our time learning the solutions to problems or the answers to questions. All other answers are incorrect, and the person who has the right answer most often is considered the best student. After years of learning the right way, we carry this type of thinking into our jobs and other areas of our lives. When we learn how to do a job, it becomes the way to do the job. Any other approaches need not be considered. If someone else does the job differently, they must be doing it incorrectly.

When it comes to work, this type of thinking can really hurt us. Rigid, inflexible thinking keeps us from finding novel, creative, simpler and better ways to do the job.

If you ever found the one best way to do a job, how would you know you had found it? The fact is that you wouldn't. Solutions to problems are not absolute. Sweeping a floor with a broom is a good solution to the debris problem, compared to picking up dirt by hand, but what if a vacuum cleaner is available? A good rule of thumb is that there are always at least two good ways to do anything.

⊙⊙ 10. 'MORE DISCIPLINE MEANS LESS FREEDOM'

In the process of growing up, we are introduced to various forms of discipline. As a small child you sat at a desk arranged in a row with other desks. You weren't allowed to talk. You had to sit there unless given permission to get up. You had to come home at a certain time and be in bed at a certain hour, perhaps when you weren't tired. Perhaps you may have been exposed to another type of discipline, that of the military services. In basic training, you were locked up, stripped of your personal identity and forced to conform to exacting standards of behaviour.

With experiences such as these for reference, it's no surprise that the word 'discipline' often has carried a negative connotation. Even though we may, in retrospect, believe it was beneficial for us, our gut-level feelings associate discipline with a loss of personal freedom. Thus, we conclude that disciplining ourselves is done at the expense of limiting our freedom. We tend to think of freedom and discipline as representing two ends of a continuum: more of one means less of the other. If we step back and view freedom and discipline objectively, it becomes obvious that this is not the case. Freedom and discipline are not trade-offs. They can exist in various combinations.

---◆---

Low freedom and little discipline.
Examples of this are high-crime areas of our cities where
you can't walk the streets for fear of your life.

High freedom and little discipline.
Life on a tropical island where the living is easy
would be an example of this.

Low freedom and high discipline.
We are all familiar with this combination. Examples
are prisons and autocratic governments.

High freedom and great great discipline.
This occurs when people impose self-discipline. They set their own
goals, formulate a strategy and impose order on themselves. They
program themselves to satisfy their own needs. They learn to make
the most of their time and energy and, as a result, they work less
and accomplish more.

---◆ — ◆ — ◆---

🔲 11. 'JUSTICE FOR ALL'

Life is not fair and never will be. There are numerous times when life deals us a bad hand. You did the work and someone else took all the credit. That's not fair. Someone else gets the promotion because she's friendlier with the boss. That's not fair. Your boss screws up, lays the blame at your feet and you get fired. That's not fair. You work twice as hard as your neighbour and are twice as smart, but you earn half the income. That's not fair. The possibilities for injustice are infinite.

Life owes us nothing. Yet most of us behave as though we signed a contract before birth guaranteeing us a fair deal. When things don't go our way, we waste time and energy lamenting the injustice done to us: 'That's not fair!'; 'I got screwed!'; 'If it weren't for them!'; 'Would I do that to you?'; 'I get all the bad breaks'.

It is also easy to utilise injustice as a cop-out. The reasoning is simple. What's the use of trying if life is nothing but bad breaks? Thus, in addition to wasting time over past misfortunes, we deal ourselves a second blow by becoming immobilised. We simply give up.

The justice myth is overcome by acknowledging that jus-tice simply doesn't exist. Justice, like beauty, is in the eye of the beholder. When fate is unkind to you, recognise the misfortune for what it is and resolve to learn something from it that will help you in the future. Then promptly get back in the ring. Becoming immobile and wallowing in self-pity is not a consequence of being badly done by. Rather, it is an irrational choice some of us make from time to time.

It's an unjust world, and there are no guarantees that you will make it if you try. However, one thing is certain: you won't make it if you don't try.

🔲 12. 'WE WORK BEST UNDER PRESSURE'

Many of us like to believe that we do our best work under pressure. However, a closer look generally reveals that this is a type of wishful thinking used to justify procrastination. The rationalisation goes something like this: 'Because I work better when the pressure is really on, I'll wait until the last minute. That will really get me psyched up. Then I'll turn on the after-burners, give it all I've got and do a superior job.' It's a superb and common form of self-delusion.

Few of us ever do our best work under pressure, despite what we would like to believe. Before subjecting yourself to pressure in the future, you should consider the following potential consequences:

◆ If you are forced to work at an accelerated pace, you increase the odds of making mistakes. If you do make a crucial mistake, you may not have time to correct it.

◆ Pressure situations makes you extremely vulnerable to Murphy's Law: Nothing is as easy as it looks. Everything takes longer than you expect. And if anything can go wrong, it will — at the worst possible moment!

Something may come up that's extremely urgent and rob you of those few precious moments you allocated to doing the job. You wait until the night before to write that important report for the boss, and the roof starts to leak, or your spouse gets sick, or the computer breaks down. As a result, you end up not doing the job or botching it so badly that you have to start all over again. If you didn't have time to do it right the first time, where are you going to find the time to do it again?

◆ Assuming all went well and you did get a lot done in a short time, it only means you know how to be effective but don't choose to unless you are under pressure. You are cheating yourself by failing to become more of what you are capable of.

◆ If you don't get the job done and you could have done it by starting earlier, you will probably suffer a loss of confidence and self-esteem. Who needs that?

Turn Off Those Tapes

When you allow irrational beliefs such as the 12 examples just given to govern your behaviour, your time and energy are channelled into unproductive efforts. Therefore, a giant step towards working smarter is to identify any irrational beliefs about work you may be clinging to, get them out in the open and see them for what they are. Irrational thoughts must be consciously exposed before you can work on banishing them from your life.

Start replacing those old ideas that don't work with ones that do. Turn off those old worn-out tapes and replace them with viable programs designed to increase your awareness, flexibility and productivity. It's not easy. It involves recognition, motivation and change. It means making some difficult decisions and then disciplining yourself to do what needs to be done until you have accomplished your task. Only you can know if it's worth the effort. Only you can be responsible for you, and only you will know the joy you will get from the accomplishment.

To give yourself a motivational boost, you <u>need to create desire within yourself.</u> You can do this by thinking big. By thinking of the finer things you will do. The great accomplishments. The richer life that will be yours. We know there are great opportunities waiting. We know they can be our opportunities if we will but take the first step to grasp them, and thinking big is the first step. If we then follow through with an earnest routine of steady and effective daily work and study, the opportunities can be ours.

Tomorrow, we say to ourselves. Tomorrow we will get started for sure. Tomorrow we will put that new idea to work, or tomorrow we will change our routine to enable more to be done in the hours available. Tomorrow there will be time. Tomorrow I will work smarter. But tomorrow becomes today and we are still on the same old road, doing the same things we always do that so far have only produced ordinary results. We are slaves on the treadmill of our habits.

We attend meetings, seminars and conventions. We hear how others have made the change. How their lives have been enriched by performance, and we plan. We plan to change tomorrow. Tomorrow we will start, always tomorrow. The sadness of our tomorrows that never come. The waste of our promised tomorrows. But this book is about today, not tomorrow. It's about what we can do now.

I want you to start today, while you are reading this book. I want you to start by adopting the concept of thinking big as a way of life. For there is a marvellous magic generated by thinking big, by practising everlasting optimism in the midst of pessimism and doubt. I challenge you to think big, to plan big and to act big. Remember always to think big — not about problems, but about positive possibilities. <u>Think big — not about obstacles,</u> but about opportunities; be <u>receptive to change, to new ideas,</u> especially those changes and ideas that confront you today. Take advantage of them, work on them, step off the treadmill of habit and take charge of your life. To have free choice and not exercise it is to deny opportunity. Today is your opportunity. Don't miss it on the promise of tomorrow.

CHAPTER 2

IT'S YOUR LIFE — GOALS OF THE GAME

If you really know what things you want out of life, it's amazing how opportunities will come to enable you to carry them out.
JOHN M GODDARD

HUMAN BEINGS ARE naturally goal-seeking creatures. When we have no goals, we live an aimless and purposeless life. The next time someone tells you they feel life is not worthwhile or that they are bored, take a closer look. What they are really saying is that they have no worthwhile problems to solve, obstacles to conquer or goals to achieve.

Developing a successful plan for effectiveness begins with goal-setting. You can make a very good case that goals, and the sense of purpose that accompanies them, are necessary for survival. Actuaries report high incidences of poor health and death shortly after the mandatory retirement age. After 40 or 50 years in a job or career, it is understandable that many people may sometimes feel stripped of their sense of direction and value when retirement is thrust upon them. Many of us reach retirement totally unprepared, with no other goals to pursue, and as a result we rust out rather than wear out.

Compare the retirement syndrome with the fact that many creative people such as artists and composers often enjoy much greater than average longevity. Many live well into their eighties and nineties, and their final years are often the most productive. Unlike most of us, they die with their boots on. Am I saying that artists tend to live longer because they are more creative? That's not the point at all. Rather, I believe that longevity is attributable to a sense of purpose and direction. To these people, there is always another symphony to compose or canvas to fill.

We can't all be artists, but we all need and can have goals. Of course, we all have some goals. However, most of them are vague and poorly conceived. Few of us ever undertake the task of setting some definite goals for our lives, and yet doing this would greatly increase the odds of our working less and accomplishing more. Until we decide what we want, we aren't very likely to get it. In the meantime, we fritter away our lives by working more and accomplishing less.

GUIDELINES FOR SETTING GOALS

We all recognise the importance of goals. However, when it comes to the task of setting specific goals, we often back off or procrastinate. We feel uneasy about it. Planning our life seems like such an onerous task that we simply throw up our hands and say, in effect, 'I just don't know where to begin.' Many people who attend my seminars on goal achievement say to me afterwards, 'I think I know what to do, but I don't know what I want.' This is a sign of either a very satisfied individual, or of someone who is unwilling to make a strong commitment and accept the responsibility for their own success or failure.

Here is a program that will provide the structure you need to get you started on your way to meaningful goal-setting. If you follow these instructions and guidelines, the task of goal-setting will become far less burdensome. In fact, you will probably enjoy it. The more important task of achieving the goals we set will be dealt with at the end of this chapter.

An Exercise in Self-discovery

It makes little sense to decide what you want out of life until you have
a good idea of who you are. This is why the following self-discovery
exercise precedes goal-setting. Once you have established a sense of
who you are, you will be in a better position to set meaningful goals.

Take 10 index cards. On one side of each card write the following
incomplete statement: My name is (your name) and I am a(n)____.
Now complete each statement differently. Work rapidly (spend no
more than about a minute on each), as the objective of this exercise is
to discover your true feelings about yourself. Don't censor any
answers that come to mind. Write them down. Answers such as
gambler, alcoholic or ping-pong fiend are no less valid than answers
like human being, parent, student, wife, homeowner or sports fan.

You may find you need more than 10 cards. That's fine. Use as many
as you need. Some people find it difficult to come up with
10 answers. This is generally because they are censoring their
thoughts. If you encounter this problem, perform this exercise when
you are alone and won't be disturbed. Most of all, remember that
there are no right or wrong answers. The key is spontaneity.

When you have completed all 10 statements, read them over, arrange
them in order of their importance to you and number them. Then turn
over the first card and complete the following statement: 'This "I am"
is first because ____.' Do the same for the remaining cards, in order.

Now take a moment to look over your self-discovery cards and reflect
on them. Imagine that the cards were written by someone else,
and write down your answers to the following questions:

1. What do these cards tell you about this person?

2. What things are most important to them?

3. What types of things would this person enjoy
doing with their life that they aren't doing?

4. How would you recommend this person spend their life
if they had only six months to live?

Keep the self-discovery cards and your answers to the questions nearby. You will want to refer to them as you formulate your goals.

Setting Your Goals

In trying to decide what you want out of life, it helps to break down your life into manageable units. In order to do that, try this exercise.

Take six more index cards or sheets of paper and label each with one of the following headings: career goals, personal relationship goals, recreational goals, personal growth goals, material goals, social goals and business goals. Next, pick up each card and write down some goals that you think you would like to achieve. As in the first exercise, work rapidly and don't censor your impulses. If you think you would like to do it, it's a potential goal.

Be sure your goals are your own! I cannot emphasise this point too strongly. It's *your* life. Take charge of it and do what's meaningful to you. If there is any one concept in this book that supersedes the importance of having goals, it is that your goals must be set by you and no one else.

Unfortunately, most of us allow our goals to be set by our employers, parents, spouses, children, or even the government. It's far more difficult to set your own goals and be your own person when there exists a myriad of forces persuading you to do otherwise.

Setting your own goals and striving to achieve them is a major step towards personal freedom and a meaningful life. This doesn't preclude your doing what others want you to do or soliciting suggestions from others about what your goals should be. In fact, talking and listening to friends or relatives who know you well may trigger some meaningful goals you wouldn't have thought of alone. But the final decision on your goals must be yours. As Christopher Morley, the American novelist and essayist, said, 'There is only one success — to be able to spend your life in your own way.'

At this point you may be thinking that all this talk about setting your own goals is interesting but somewhat unrealistic. When I discuss the importance of self-set goals in seminars, a common response is, 'Sure, I'd like to open my own business, or go back to university, or live somewhere else, or change careers, but I have to face reality.' Then I hear a number of excuses, such as I'm too old, my spouse would leave me, my parents are getting old, I have to think about my children and so on. This kind of reasoning is little more than a fear of failure and an attempt to cling to security in a world where there is none. The closest we can get to security is in our own ability to perform, plus a strong 'can do' self-image. When we support this kind of thinking with a goal-oriented philosophy, we greatly increase our chances of success.

Kevan Gosper (Order of Australia) is an outstanding example of the value of personal goal-setting. Kevan has excelled in both sport and business. A former Olympian and Commonwealth Games medalist, he has applied the same commitment and determination to his corporate career. A former chairman of the board and chief executive officer with Shell Australia, he is now a cabinet member of the International Olympic Council, the governing board of the Olympics. An outstanding achiever by any measure.

Kevan says, have faith in yourself, decide what you want, listen to others but make your own decisions. When you have decided on your goal, work with a single purpose to achieve it. If you really want to win, you have to give it your very best. Above all, make sure the goal is yours and remember that *you* decide the limits of your success.

Listed below are examples of specific goals which you may have. I don't mean to imply that any of these should or should not be your goals. They are included merely for the purpose of illustration. If you think of a goal that falls into more than one category, write it down on each appropriate card. A goal that appears several times is usually a good one for you, because it indicates a wide range of potential satisfaction.

CAREER GOALS

- Become managing director of the company by age 40.
- Get promoted this year.
- Find another career more in line with my tastes and aptitudes.
- Open my own restaurant.
- Become the top sales representative in my district.

- Get my boss's job.
- Get a job with my company's competitor.
- Start a business of my own.

BUSINESS GOALS

- Increase net profit by ___ per cent by __ / __ /__ (date).
- Decrease costs by ___ per cent by __ / __ /__ .
- Open a new branch by __ / __ /__ .
- Buy out my competitor by __ / __ /__ .
- Increase the sales force by ___ per cent by __ / __ /__ .
- Increase annual turnover by ___ per cent by __ / __ /__ .

PERSONAL RELATIONSHIP GOALS

- Devote two hours each day to getting to know my children better.
- Take one escape weekend every three months with my partner.
- Try to meet at least one new person each day.
- Convert a former adversary to a friend.
- Fall in love.
- Get married.
- Get a divorce.
- Cultivate one new, close friendship each month.
- Learn to remember names.

RECREATIONAL GOALS

- Find a better way to relax each day.
- Go on a safari.
- Learn how to abseil.
- Get on the Internet and talk to people around the world.
- Buy a boat.
- Write a book.
- Take a trip to China.
- Lower my golf handicap by five strokes.
- Sleep late on Saturdays.

◆ Watch the sunset.
◆ Take up painting.

PERSONAL GROWTH GOALS

◆ Learn one new word each day.
◆ Take a speed-reading course.
◆ Learn to make better use of my time and energy.
◆ Attend a lecture each month on a something I know little about.
◆ Learn to control my temper.
◆ Take up conversational French.
◆ Get a degree in ____.
◆ Volunteer for charity work.
◆ Give a talk on ____.

MATERIAL GOALS

◆ Be financially independent in five years.
◆ Buy a house this year.
◆ Get a sports car.
◆ Buy the best available compact disc player.
◆ Buy a motorcycle.
◆ Buy a yacht and live on it.
◆ Acquire rental property.
◆ Add another bathroom to the house.
◆ Earn enough money to pay off the mortgage.
◆ Earn an extra $ ____ a month.

SOCIAL GOALS

◆ Join the ____ club.
◆ Graduate with honours.
◆ Wear expensive clothes.
◆ Move to an impressive neighbourhood.
◆ Throw formal dinner parties for important people.
◆ Be captain of the football team.

Be sure to refer back to your self-discovery cards as you begin to write down your goals. They will be a great help in pointing the way towards which goals will be most meaningful. If, for example, one of your self-discovery cards says, 'I am a father', logical goals might be to set aside more time each week for getting better acquainted with your children or adding a family recreation room to your house. If one of your cards says, 'I am a golfer', then saving for a new set of clubs or resolving to lower your handicap by five strokes by the end of the year might be potential goals. The idea is to use the self-discovery cards as a guide to which things in life are most meaningful to you.

The reason for putting goals in writing is twofold. First, writing down your goals will help you to identify more clearly what you want. Most of us never write down our goals. We are simply content to think about them. However, thoughts are fleeting and if our goals are merely thoughts, we run a high risk of having little more than daydreams. Written goals are less likely to be forgotten or lost in the shuffle of daily routines.

Writing down goals also increases your personal commitment to them. As you take the time to think about your life and what you want out of it, you are applying the investment theory of work to planning. This is an investment of your time which has one of the highest potential payoffs. Making the effort to write down your goals means giving more of yourself to a goal than merely thinking about it. And the degree of commitment you have to a goal is the single most important factor in achieving it.

When you have completed your list, you will have the first rough draft of your goals. Setting goals is much like writing an essay or a report. You begin by putting a few ideas down on paper and then set about the task of refining, polishing and shaping them into a cohesive entity. The following guidelines are designed to help you transform your ideas about what you would like to do into a cohesive plan for getting the most from your life.

Set Challenging but Attainable Goals

Some years ago, an experiment in achievement motivation was undertaken with about 15 people who were invited to participate in a game of quoits. The spike was placed at one end of the room and each player was given several quoits to toss on to the spike. Each player was allowed to stand as far from the spike as he wished when throwing his quoits. Those players who stood close to the spike hit the target with ease and quickly lost interest. Some players stood far away, failed to make any ringers and quickly became discouraged. However, a few players stood far enough away to make the game challenging but close enough for success to be attainable. The experimenters interpreted this as a sign that these people had a high degree of achievement motivation. High achievers are usually hooked on getting satisfaction by continually setting challenging but attainable goals.

Achievement motivation experts such as David McClelland believe that the need to achieve can be learned. One major step is to set a goal that you believe you can achieve but which also causes you to stretch your abilities.

As you search through your goals cards, seek out those goals that are attainable and challenging. Unattainable goals aren't goals — they are fantasies. What is an attainable goal is a decision that only you can make. If you think you can do it and it seems right, then it's attainable and I urge you to pursue it.

Make Your Goals as Specific and Measurable as Possible

The more specific you make your goals, the more direction they will provide for you. For example, if your goal is to buy a house, start by clarifying what you have in mind. What size house? How many storeys? How many bedrooms? Brick or timber? What size block? Located where? What price range? and so on. If your goal is to be financially independent, calculate how much money you will have to acquire. The amount of money necessary for financial independence is a very personal decision. For some, $100 000 is plenty, whereas for others $1 million isn't enough.

Not all goals are as easy to measure as income or housing specifications. Goals such as being a good parent or a responsible citizen cannot easily be quantified. In these cases, you can construct a rating scale from 1 to 10, with 1 representing the poorest and 10 the ultimate. Then you can estimate where on the scale you think you are now and decide where you would like to be.

If you don't feel a rating scale is appropriate, you can always try verbally describing what you want as vividly as you can. For example, if your goal is to improve your appearance, answer questions such as, 'What can I do to my hair, skin, teeth, eyes, weight and dress in order to improve my appearance?' This will give you much more direction than simply saying, 'I want to look better.'

If you find that you cannot quantify, measure, rate or describe something, you probably can forget it as a goal.

Check Your Goals for Compatibility

In the process of setting your goals, it is possible to set two or more goals where the attainment of one prevents the attainment of the other(s). You may want to be a sales manager but don't want to give up the personal freedom you have as a sales representative. You may want to be the best in your profession (which frequently requires working long hours and weekends), but you also want to spend more time with your family. You may want to take an overseas holiday this year, but the house needs a new roof and you can't afford both. These are common examples of incompatible goals.

Or you may pour your time and energy into several projects, only to find that you can't complete them all. Goal incompatibility can lead to uncertainty and indecision about which goals to pursue. Often the result is that you pursue no goals at all. Examine your goals for incompatibility at the outset. This may save you a great deal of time and frustration later.

Keep Your Goals Flexible

Many of us shy away from writing down our goals because we feel that putting them on paper is tantamount to carving them in stone. This is an idea that needs to be dispelled here and now. As a viable, growing person, your needs and values will be evolving forever. Consequently, you will have to re-evaluate and often modify, discard or replace some of your goals. If you don't do this to some degree, then you aren't giving much thought to where you are going, or you may be thinking of goals as rigid and inflexible.

A good plan is like a comfortable shoe: it serves its purpose and flexes to accommodate the needs of the user. Keep this in mind when setting and evaluating your goals.

Set Target Dates

A good rule to impose on yourself is this: a goal doesn't become a goal until you have a deadline for accomplishment. Target dates for goal achievement are another step in increasing your motivation and commitment. When you have a major goal to accomplish, break it down into subgoals and put deadlines on them. As you meet subgoal target dates, you will feel the satisfaction and pride that comes with meaningful progress. This in turn will create even greater momentum towards achieving your major goals. Target dates, like goals, should be realistic. To help you set realistic target dates, let's divide our goals into key categories.

◆

Lifetime goals.
These are results that you wish
to accomplish or things you want to experience
in your lifetime. Often, though not necessarily,
these goals are long-range and take more
than a year to accomplish.

Intermediate goals.
These are goals you wish to accomplish
within the next year.

Daily goals.
These goals ensure that you make
the most of each day.

◆ — ◆ — ◆

All of these goals must be considered in light of each other. The daily goals should contribute to the achievement of intermediate goals. Likewise, intermediate goals should be set to contribute to lifetime goals. The objective is to co-ordinate your use of time and energy for maximum effectiveness. The concept of co-ordinating a hierarchy of goals is called goal congruency. As you place your goals in a time perspective, you may want to modify, add to or reject some of them in the interests of goal congruency. Most of us don't do this. When we fail to relate our todays to our tomorrows, we find ourselves starting from scratch each day. We are left with the grim realisation that our wheels are spinning but we aren't going anywhere. Let's not have this happen to you.

SETTING LIFETIME GOALS

Establishing your lifetime goals is a tall order. The following exercise will help you to clarify them. You will want to update your lifetime goals list periodically. As you mature, you may expect goals to be added and deleted from your list. As was pointed out earlier, good planning is flexible.

Take a sheet of paper and label it 'Lifetime Goals'. Based on what you have written, you should have little trouble in coming up with a number of goals. Many of them will be very broad. That's okay. The purpose of lifetime goals is to provide a general direction for your life. To believe you can plan your entire lifetime in specific detail is unrealistic. Your intermediate goals will be more specific, and daily goals should be the most specific of all.

LIFETIME GOALS

Own a house.

Travel the world.

Be happy and healthy.

Have a successful career.

Save for a comfortable retirement.

SETTING INTERMEDIATE GOALS — PROJECT PLANNING

Most of us think of intermediate goals as projects — things we would like to accomplish in the foreseeable future, usually within the next year. Projects can bridge the gap between lifetime goals and daily activities. The following project-planning exercise will help you clarify your intermediate goals.

List your intermediate goals.
Take a sheet of paper for each goal,
and answer the following questions:

1. State clearly and specifically a goal you would like
to achieve in the next six months.

2. Why do you want to achieve this goal?

3. If you succeed, what will it do for you?

4. How much do you want to achieve this goal?

5. How will achieving this goal contribute to
the attainment of your lifetime goals?

6. What price will you have to pay to achieve this goal?
Are you willing to pay it?

7. Estimate your chances of achieving this goal.

8. What will happen if you fail?

9. List the major subgoals involved in achieving this goal
and assign a target date to each.

10. What obstacles stand between you and successful completion
of your project? How will you overcome them?

11. What can you do today that will start you on the path
to achieving this goal?

SETTING DAILY GOALS — THE TO-DO LIST

Those of you who habitually set daily goals know the value of the daily to-do list. A well-known story about the efficacy of a to-do list concerns Charles Schwab when he was president of Bethlehem Steel in the United States. He called in Ivy Lee, a consultant, and said, 'Show me a way to get more things done with my time, and I'll pay you any fee within reason.'

'Fine,' Lee replied. 'I'll give you something in 20 minutes that will step up your output at least 50 per cent.'

With that, Lee handed Schwab a blank piece of paper and said, 'Write down the six most important tasks that you have to do tomorrow and number them in order of their importance. Now put this paper in your pocket, and the first thing tomorrow morning look at item one and start working on it until you finish it. Then do item two, and so on. Do this until quitting time and don't be concerned if you have finished only one or two. Then on tomorrow's list put the uncompleted items at the top of the list and add your next most important tasks to the list until you have your six most important tasks on your list each day. Do this every working day. If a task is on your list for more than a week, forget it — you are only playing games. This way you will always be working on the most important ones first. If you can't finish them all by this method, you couldn't have by any other method either; and without some system you'd probably not even have decided which was the most important.'

Then Lee said, 'Try this system every working day. After you've convinced yourself of the value of the system, have your men try it. Try it as long as you wish and then send me a cheque for what you think it's worth.'

Several weeks later, Schwab sent Lee a cheque for $25 000 with a note proclaiming the advice the most profitable he had ever followed. This concept helped Schwab to earn $100 million and to turn Bethlehem Steel into one of the biggest independent steel producer in the world.

You may think Schwab was foolish to pay $25 000 for such a simple piece of advice. However, he considered the consulting fee one of his best investments. 'Sure, it was a simple idea,' he said. 'But what ideas are not basically simple? For the first time, my entire team and myself are getting first things done first.'

You, too, can profit by setting a daily to-do list. The small amount of time and effort you invest in this will repay you many times over. Make this practice as habitual as brushing your teeth or having your morning cup of coffee. Here's how it's done.

1. Make a list of all the things you want to accomplish today.

2. Now rank them in order of importance.

3. Carry the list with you wherever you go.

4. Cross off items on your list as you do them.

5. Add any items not crossed off to the next day's to-do list or reconsider their importance.

SETTING PRIORITIES — THE 80/20 RULE

If you carried out the exercises on goal-setting previously described, you probably had little trouble in coming up with many goals. In fact, you probably have enough goals to last you several lifetimes. However, the simple fact is that you have only one life. You are now faced with the prospect of setting priorities and deciding which goals are most important to your overall happiness and fulfilment. Setting priorities is simply a matter of putting first things first.

The simplest system for setting priorities is to rank goals in order of importance, as Charles Schwab did on his to-do list. Other people, such as time-management consultant Alan Lakein, use the A, B, C method. Goals are first put into three categories:

A. Must do

B. Should do

C. Nice to do.

Then each set of goals is ranked in order. Thus your top-priority item is labelled A–1. The idea is to start with As, and to do only Cs if you complete all the As and Bs.

It makes little difference which type of priority system you use, as long as it works for you. I find that the simple numbering system works for me. Others enjoy being creative and colour-code their lists. Top-priority items are underlined in red, medium-priority in blue and so on.

The 80/20 rule, or Pareto principle (named after Vilfredo Pareto, a 19th century Italian economist), explains why setting priorities is so important in securing effectiveness. This rule states that 80 per cent of the value of a group of items is generally concentrated in only 20 per cent of the items. It's an interesting concept, and there are plenty of examples in life that tend to validate the 80/20 rule. Eighty per cent of the dollar value of an inventory is often found in 20 per cent of the items. Eighty per cent of all telephone calls come from 20 per cent of the callers. Eighty per cent of the meals ordered in a restaurant consist of 20 per cent of the items on the menu. Eighty per cent of all television viewing is spent watching 20 per cent of all programs. If you keep the 80/20 rule in mind, you will find it appearing in many different places.

However, our use of the 80/20 rule applies to goals. Simply put, it means you can be 80 per cent effective by achieving 20 per cent of your goals. If you have a daily to-do list of 10 items, this means you can generally expect to be 80 per cent effective by successfully completing only the two most important items on your list! How's that for good news? The main idea is that to be effective, you must concentrate on the most important items first.

HOW TO ACHIEVE YOUR GOALS

Having dealt with setting goals, we have covered the 'want to' of goal-achieving. Now we must deal with the most crucial issue in achieving goals, the 'how to', because this is where 90 per cent of all good intentions come unstuck. You want to increase your earnings by $10 000 a year. How are you going to do it? You want to be financially independent in five years. How are you going to do it? You want to increase the net profit of your business by 25 per cent this year. Fine, it's an excellent goal, but how are you going to do it?

Almost everyone I know can set goals, which is the 'want to'. What mostly makes the difference between those who succeed and those who fail, is the 'how to'. Most people never really get beyond the 'want to' stage, yet the only worthwhile issue is 'how to'.

Why Goals are Important

We are essentially goal-oriented. We have a natural goal-seeking mechanism within us which we carry all our lives. Failure to understand the necessity to develop goals which we can seek and achieve, and therefore satisfy our natural urge to compete, severely limits our performance. On the other hand, when we strive for and achieve goals, we set up the ultimate motivational climate within which we are most likely to achieve our potential.

In order to satisfy our deepest motivational and psychological urges, we need to have a system of goal-getting which will make it possible for us to perform at our highest individual level and to consistently succeed in what we attempt.

The world is full of people who set goals and have no real commitment to getting them. Much of the reason behind setting and not getting goals lies in the fact that the individuals concerned simply do not understand the factors which most influence their chances of getting the goals they set. In order to become champion goal-getters rather than just goal-setters, we have to do three things effectively:

1. Manage our minds and our motivation
2. Use time effectively
3. Write down the 'how to' of getting our goals.

MANAGING OUR MIND

What we think is very important. All we have and all we are, is our thoughts. There is nothing other than what we think about. The world to you and me is the reality of what we think about. We can create the world we want by the pattern of our thoughts. Life will be as beautiful as we can imagine. We will be as successful as we imagine. We will be as rich as we think we should be. Remember, in some marvellous way which we do not understand, vividly imagined events, supported by purposeful action and sustained by faith, come to pass.

Dominant Thinking

As humans, we achieve our dominant thought. That is the way our mind works, and it is important that we understand this because it is a crucial factor in how to achieve our goals. For example, if your current dominant thought was to be somewhere else, doing something else, you wouldn't be reading this book. It is crucial to achieving our goals that we understand this principle and apply it by making our goals our dominant thought.

We Cannot Move Away
— Only Towards

We need also to understand, because it is most important in terms of achieving our goals, that we cannot move away from that which we do not want, or want to become; we can only move towards what it is we want, or want to become. As an example, we cannot move away from being poor; we can only move towards being rich. We cannot move away from being unhappy; we can only move towards being happy. We cannot move away from failure; we can only move towards success. We cannot move away from being fat; we can only move towards being thin. This is because we achieve our dominant thought. If we focus on being poor, for example, then that becomes our dominant thought and we will achieve our dominant thought and stay poor. If we want to become rich, we have to focus on what we want, which is to be rich, not on what we want to avoid, which is being poor.

Patterns of Thinking

I know many people who genuinely want to become rich and who try hard to become rich, but whose thought pattern keeps them poor. For example, in the mornings they wake up, throw back the covers, and their thought patterns run something like this: 'I wish I weren't poor. If only I could have a bigger house, a bigger boat, go on longer holidays, get paid more money, earn more, have more, be more. It's not very nice being poor. Because I'm poor, I have to live like this. If only I were rich. If only they would pay me what I am worth.' Unfortunately, such people may have a genuine desire to be rich, but because of a lack of understanding of the technique of how to apply thought to get what they want out of life, they focus on 'poor'. They achieve their dominant thought and, as a result, stay poor.

If they were to get out of bed of a morning and think 'rich' — picture in their mind the house they want and the sort of income they believe they should get, make a bargain with life about what they are willing to give in return for what it is they expect to get, think rich, act rich, work rich, talk like a rich person, have mental images of a rich person and read articles on being rich — then they would become rich. They must develop mental images associated with what it is they want and focus on what they want, not on what they want to avoid. Focus on the house they want to live in, not on the one they want to leave. Focus on the income they want, not on the income they have. They must focus, focus and focus again, because if they want to be rich, being rich has to be their dominant thought. If they can't see it in their mind's eye, they can't have it.

Becoming rich is only an example. Your real goal could just as easily be a trip around the world, lowering your golf handicap by five strokes, increasing your sales by 25 per cent or learning a new language.

Programming Our Mind

We program ourselves to achieve our goals by self-talk: I can, I will, I want, I am, I shall. We achieve our goals by each day achieving our dominant thoughts. Vince Lombardi, the great American football coach, is quoted as saying, 'Success is a day-by-day, inch-by-inch struggle towards our goals.' This simply means that if we make our goal our dominant thought, then day by day and inch by inch we will make our way towards our goal, and that's what it is all about. It's as simple or as difficult as you believe it to be.

Let me ask you some questions: Are the things that you really want out of life your dominant thought? Do you know your goals? If I came to where you lived or worked, would I find them written down? Are you working on them every day of your life? Are they central to all your thinking? Are the images, desires and wants that you express those of the goals you want to attain? Are they in order of priority? Are they specific? Time bounded? Tough but achievable? If they are, your chances of achieving them are very high. Now you need to commit them to paper.

WRITING DOWN THE 'HOW TO' OF GETTING YOUR GOALS

Never forget that work in itself is not accomplishment. If it were, those who work hardest would always win, and you know that is not true. If hard work in itself was the answer, then the problems of succeeding in life would be easy to solve.

Perspiration is necessary — hard work is always on the side of those who want to win. But inspiration is essential. It is said that a drop of inspiration is worth a bucket of perspiration, so simply identifying and prioritising your goals will not accomplish your end. Most times, something more is required, and that something is the creative twist to what you are going to do in order to get what you want.

For each of your main goals, prepare a goal-getting plan like that shown on the opposite page.

1. Define your goal, e.g. 'Increase my net income by 20 per cent by __/__/__ (date).

2. Write it down in the section of the goal-getting plan headed 'Goal'.

3. In the section headed 'Measurement method', write down how you propose to measure the successful attainment of your goal.

4. Plan the activities you need to carry out in order to achieve your goal. This is the heart of the method. Stay with it until you know how you are going to achieve your goal. Write your activities in sequential order commencing with 1. Place the number in the column headed 'Item'.

Write the activity you plan to do in the column headed 'Activities'.

In this section, pay special attention to creative thinking. Ask yourself: Am I doing anything different?

When you have completed your list of activities, do the following.

5. Decide the date on which you will finish each activity. Write the date down under the heading 'Date to be completed'.

6. Give your plan a priority number.

7. Make your activity list your daily work plan. Write the activities on your to-do list.

8. As you complete each planned activity, sign it off in the column headed 'Date completed'.

Keep working at your plan. If you do, goal-getting will become as easy as goal-setting.

GOAL-GETTING PLAN

GOAL		PRIORITY

MEASUREMENT METHOD

ITEM	ACTIVITIES	DATE TO BE COMPLETED	DATE COMPLETED

WHY PUTTING YOUR GOALS IN WRITING IS IMPORTANT

Putting your goals in writing, and working out 'how to' achieve them is of key importance. The real issue isn't what we want; it's how to get what we want.

You may ask why it is necessary to write down the activities; the answer, of course, is because it is much easier than trying to keep track of them in your head. Let's try a simple exercise. You have, say, six goals you want to achieve. Each of them will require from 10 to 15 activities to ensure that you achieve the goal. Each of the activities to be undertaken will need to be done in sequence. Some will need to be done by someone other than yourself. Many will be mini-goals in themselves; and each of the activities, if you are to succeed, needs to be accomplished by a set time. So now you have 90 activities, all to be carried out in sequence. You need to know who's going to do them and in what order. Do you really believe that you, or anyone else, could keep track of 90 activities in your head? I usually ask this question at my seminars, and I have yet to come across one person who thought they could do so.

What are the Alternatives?

You basically have two alternatives:

- ◆ Be positive. Write down your goals and your 'how to' lists.
- ◆ Don't write your goals down; just carry out tasks as they occur to you.

Which alternative do you think would be the most effective? In 20 years I have not had anyone at my seminars say that carrying out tasks as they thought of them would be more effective, but I constantly hear the statement: 'If I write them down, I will only have to alter them in the future.'

Of course some goals will need to be altered. Altering your goals is no problem. Changing your mind is no problem. Things will change. You will change. You may even abandon some of them, but *you* will always be in charge. When the necessity arises for you to change a goal, you will know what you are altering it from and what you are altering it to. Whether you carry out activities day-by-day or write them down, if you change your mind you will have to make allowances and do different activities.

PLANNING YOUR GOALS

How long is it since you took an hour, two hours, a day or even a whole week to sit down and plan your goals as if your life really counted? Sadly, the answer in most cases will be that you have never done it. Does this mean you cannot succeed without doing it? No, it doesn't. There are more roads to Rome than one. There are more ways than one to do things. I am not claiming this is the only way. I am saying that if you want to win more often, win more, do it easier, quicker, be more in charge and have fewer problems, then plan what you want to do. Write down your plan and get started on achieving it.

My good friend Kim Harding is a classic example of someone who uses the techniques discussed in this chapter. Kim is a young woman with great purpose and outstanding accomplishments. She has received more than 30 international and Australian awards for excellence in marketing. Today she heads up her own very successful consulting business, called Pin Point, a very apt title for one so goal-oriented.

Kim says, 'I always write down my goals. I do this mostly at the end of the year to get ready for the new year, but I do them anytime the need arises. When I am doing my end-of-year review and rewrite of my goals, I spend up to a week getting them right. Then I keep them in my diary, constantly in view. At the end of each month I review my progress and write further action plans. Each day I take part of the action plans and put them on my to-do list and do them. If necessary, I make changes as I go.'

Kim said she sets goals in the following categories: self-achievement, financial, career, social and society (to give back some of her success). One of her strong beliefs is that we should let our dreams lead us to our goals. Kim uses a biography technique to show the way to her plans. She has written her biography to age 70. That way she sees her future and fills it in as she goes. Kim says this technique works very well for her.

Let me give you another example. Recently in the United States, a survey was carried out on the productivity of 30 high achievers. All were very successful, being multi-millionaires and first-class achievers. When questioned, only six of those surveyed admitted to writing down their plans. The response indicated that you do not have to write your goals down to be successful. The researchers then asked the respondents what they had achieved. They checked the total productivity of the group and discovered that the 24 who didn't write down their plans had achieved only 40 per cent of the group's total achievement. The six who had written down their plans had achieved 60 per cent of the total of the group's achievement. This result is proof enough for me that writing down your plans is more effective than trying to keep track of them in your head.

If you want to be a champion at managing your life and achieving your goals, if you want to work smarter not harder, if you want to work less and have more time for yourself and your family, if you want to get more and get it quicker, if you want to do more and do it more effectively, then write down the 'how to' of your plans.

Whether you will ever successfully carry out all the activities you have defined will be decided by the extent of your desire to achieve your goal. The main factor in motivation is desire. When an individual desires, above everything else, to achieve a particular goal, then that desire will push their motivation towards working and doing what needs to be done to ensure that they achieve their goal. Nothing will be too difficult. They will try and try again until they achieve success.

If your desire to achieve is strong, if your motivation is high, if your goals are your dominant thinking, all you have to do is write down your goals in a plan of action and then carry out your plan.

REMEMBER

Effectiveness is the key to it all.

Your most valuable resource is time,
make the most of it.

Think big. Don't obsess over problems
or things you can't change.

Focus on the positive possibilities
and opportunities of given situations.

Developing a successful plan
for effectiveness begins with goal-setting.

It's your life. Take charge of it
and set some goals and work
towards achieving them.

PART 2

LAUNCHING
YOURSELF

CHAPTER 3

GETTING ORGANISED

> A *place for everything,*
> and *everything in its place.*
> SAMUEL SMILES

IN ONE OF his films, W C Fields plays an executive whose desk top is a morass of clutter. In one scene he returns to his desk to find that an efficiency expert has organised, rearranged and streamlined everything on it. The desk top is now a picture of neatness and efficiency, but Fields is frustrated. He can't find anything! So he vigorously throws the neat stacks of paper up in the air, tossing them in the way a gourmet would a salad. Then he backs off, surveys the desk top with satisfaction, deftly reaches into the pile and pulls out the desired document.

To fully appreciate the satire of that scene, we should place it in historical perspective. At the time when Fields was in his glory, efficiency experts were preaching the gospel of organisation. One of the cardinal sins of inefficiency was to have a desk that had anything on top of it other than the immediate work at hand. A clear desk was heralded as the badge of efficiency and productivity.

Today we are less sure of this. Certainly, an organised life is usually a great deal more effective than a chaotic one. Most of us could enhance our effectiveness with more organisation. However, hard-and-fast rules are not the order of the day when it comes to organising. This is what Fields was trying to tell us in the film. We all must organise to suit our own personality and the task at hand.

As you plan your life, resist the temptation to become overly organised — it's an effectiveness killer. Most of us know someone who spends most of their time getting organised rather than focusing on high-priority issues. The same problem can arise as you try to work smarter. Remember, these ideas are merely means to an end, and that end is to increase your lifetime effectiveness. Running around with a stopwatch and keeping a totally clear desk isn't going to accomplish what you want in life.

Nevertheless, there are some good guidelines for organising your life and your thoughts, and these are discussed in this chapter. If you practise these guidelines as guidelines rather than as hard-and-fast rules, you will find they will help you to get the most from your time and effort. With that thought in mind, let's look at a few of them.

GET THE PROPER TOOLS TO DO THE JOB

Thomas Carlyle, the 19th century Scottish writer, once said, 'Man is a tool-using animal . . . without tools he is nothing, with tools he is all.' These are words worth remembering. How many times have you laboured at an unsuccessful activity only to find that having a particular tool could have saved you a great deal of time, energy and frustration? This type of experience is usually most apparent to us when we are trying to repair the family car or something around the house. This is because we tend to think of tools as tangible instruments, as many of them are. However, to make the most of this guideline we should use the word 'tool' in a much broader context.

A tool is anything you use to help you achieve your goals. No matter what your goals or what activities you pursue, all of them involve tools. If you are an accountant, then your tools include the obvious computer software, pencils, papers and calculators, as well as your degree and your practical knowledge. If you work in an office, then the office itself, with its desk, chair and floor space, is a tool.

Other examples of less obvious tools are automobiles, statistical tables, newspapers, foreign languages and interviewing techniques. The list is endless.

Before setting out to perform a task or achieve a goal, stop and ask yourself, 'What tools are necessary to complete the task successfully, and do I have them?' If you don't have the proper tools, first consider getting someone else to do the job. Your time, energy and expenses may be greatly reduced by employing someone else. However, if it's something only you can do, make an effort to first <u>equip yourself with the best tools available</u>. The difference between wise men and fools is often found in their choice of tools.

Organise Your Workspace

Consider the environment in which you will be performing the task. Organising your workspace is largely a personal matter that depends on your own tastes and the job to be done. However, there are several basic factors to keep in mind:

◆ **Location.** If you are fortunate enough to choose your workspace, choose one that is conducive to performing the task. If the job requires concentration, look for a quiet, private place. On the other hand, if you are opening your own business, choose a well-travelled location where potential customers have easy access.

◆ **Space.** After you have chosen the proper work location, measure how much space you have to work with. Most of us usually find we have less than we want. It helps to know what space is available before furnishing it with the necessary tools.

◆ **Easy access to the tools you use frequently.** It helps here to make a list of the tools you use and to rank them in order of how often you use them. You will then have a guideline for arranging them for easiest access. Refrain from cluttering your workspace with nonessential items.

◆ **Comfort.** Some people don't believe that workspaces should be designed for comfort. They are generally people who play the hard-work tape or the work-is-inherently-unpleasant tape. The fact is that discomfort is a distraction that serves only to hinder productivity. Why make things more difficult than they have to be?

A comfortable workspace generally has proper seating, ventilation and lighting. If you work sitting down for long periods, choose a firm, comfortable chair that gives good back support. Try to find one comfortable enough that you won't have to get up every 10 minutes, but not so comfortable that you will fall asleep in it. To avoid eyestrain, use indirect, uniform lighting. Take regular breaks from your computer screen. Adequate ventilation will help to prevent unnecessary fatigue from stuffiness in the work environment.

Master Your Desk

A great many of us perform some or all of our work at a desk. As I mentioned earlier, a desk is a tool — and it is one of the most abused and misused of tools. So consider the following, a desk is not:

◆ A place to conduct a paper drive. Judging from the many cluttered desk tops I have seen, I'm convinced that paper recyclers would be better supplied if they raided desk tops in office buildings.

◆ A storage depot for food or coffee mugs.

◆ A place to stack items you want to remember. A German executive once remarked to time-management expert Alec Mackenzie that desk tops get stacked because we put things there that we don't want to forget. With time, the stacks grow higher and we forget what is in each one. So we waste large amounts of time retrieving lost items and thinking about all those things we don't want to forget.

◆ A status symbol or place to display awards, trophies and the like. This mistaken use of desks causes us only to make desks larger than they have to be. With more surface area we have more room for clutter, and somehow more clutter magically appears to fill up any available space.

Now that we have discussed what a desk is *not*, let's look at what a desk *is*. It's a tool that expedites the receiving and processing of information and should be utilised with those objectives in mind.

You may have a desk and not need one. Some executives have thrown out their desks and declare that their effectiveness has increased as a result. They have replaced the standard office desk and chair with a lounge chair, clipboard, small writing table, and filing cabinets. Advocates of the deskless office have seen an improvement in face-to-face communication and an atmosphere of greater freedom. They no longer feel chained to a desk. Consider the possibility that you may not need a desk; if you can get rid of it, try working without it and see what happens.

How to Reorganise Your Desk for Effectiveness

Assuming you do need your desk, you may want to embark on a reorganisation project. If you decide to reorganise your desk, block out several hours in your schedule when you won't be interrupted, such as on a Saturday morning.

Desk reorganisation can be accomplished by the following procedure:

1. Get a large wastepaper bin.

2. Take everything off the top of the desk and empty all the drawers. Discard every item that is no longer of any use.

3. Make a list of all the remaining items that were in or on your desk and rank them in order of importance. When you consider each item, ask yourself, 'What's the worst thing that will happen if I throw this away?' If the answer isn't very bad, throw away the item and take it off the list.

4. Critically view all the non-discarded items and put only the most essential ones in your desk. Articles that you don't need immediate access to should be stored somewhere else, such as in a filing cabinet or bookcase.

5. Make a filing system in the deep drawers, with files well labelled and organised for quick and easy access. Periodically review all of your desk files and keep only the current essential ones in your desk. Over 90 per cent of all files over a year old are never referred to.

6. To use the input-output principle for processing information, get two large stacking file baskets — one to store incoming work and one for storing work you have processed and are ready to send on. Pending items of low priority or needing later attention may be filed in the desk drawer, as long as the drawers are regularly monitored.

Guidelines for Working at Your Desk

If you have gone to the trouble of reorganising your desk, you have taken a giant step towards making your desk a more effective tool. Some people find it helpful to repeat desk reorganisation every six months. The following guidelines are designed to increase your desk-work effectiveness by reducing the amount of clutter.

- Have only one project at a time on top of your desk — it should be your top priority for the moment.
- Keep items off your desk until you are ready for them. Store them in filing cabinets or drawers, but get them out of sight.

- Don't allow yourself to be sidetracked by other tasks because they are easier or more appealing. You should work on the top-priority item and keep at it until it is completed.

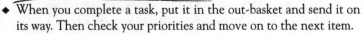

- When you complete a task, put it in the out-basket and send it on its way. Then check your priorities and move on to the next item.
- If you have one, your assistant can help by keeping your desk clear and seeing that the day's top-priority item is waiting on your desk at the beginning of each day.

These are general guidelines and they may not be suitable for you. Obsessing about a clean desk isn't going to get the job done, and for some it becomes just another detractor from effectively doing the job. Choose a style suitable for you and the work to be done, but be honest with yourself. Few of us do our best work with a heavily cluttered and disorganised desk.

Improve Your Ability to Concentrate

Concentration in any form is an amazing phenomenon. As a six year-old, I was spellbound when a friend ignited a piece of paper by focusing the sun's rays on the paper through a magnifying glass. Our own time and energy are much like the sun's rays. To the degree that we concentrate our efforts, we will succeed in getting what we want out of life. The ability to concentrate has enabled many people of modest capabilities to reach heights of success that have often eluded geniuses.

In a sense, this entire book is aimed at helping you to improve your ability to concentrate. Many of the ideas previously discussed, such as setting goals and priorities and getting the proper tools and work environment, will help you to concentrate. There are several other organisational guidelines aimed at improving your concentration.

Think with a Pencil in Your Hand

If you tried the goal-setting exercises in Chapter 2, you already have a good idea of the value of thinking on paper. When you write down your ideas, you automatically focus your full attention on them. Few, if any, of us can write one thought and think another at the same time. Thus, a pencil and paper make excellent concentration tools.

Whenever you need to concentrate, make it a habit to think with a pencil in your hand. As ideas come to you, jot them down. As you write down ideas, you will automatically be thinking them through and clarifying them in your mind. Soon you will have a list of thoughts to consider. You will be much more likely to see which ideas are irrational, erroneous or in conflict with each other if you can view them all at once.

Reserve Your Workplace Exclusively for Work

We are all creatures of habit, and most of our behaviour involves little or no thought. We learn to associate certain behaviours with a given environment. If we don't take pains to develop good habits in the work environment, all sorts of unproductive ones can develop and rob us of our time and energy.

One way to improve your ability to concentrate is to reserve your workplace only for working. For example, if you work behind a desk in an office, don't do anything at your desk that is unrelated to work. If a visitor drops in, get up and move away from the desk. If you allow yourself to socialise behind the desk, you will come to associate that location with activities other than work. When you take a break, move away from where you work. Sit in another chair or go to another room. If you develop the habit of choosing a certain spot to work, you will find yourself getting down to business much more rapidly and automatically when it's time to work.

Slow Down and Stop Constructively

One of the keys to the art of staying with a task is in knowing how and when to back off. Blind perseverance is for fools. It involves working harder, not smarter.

When you find yourself mentally blocked from solving problems, make a tactical retreat from your work. Pushing ahead will only lead to confusion and frustration. Perhaps you need to get more input about the task or need more time to digest and integrate information.

When you have to quit working, there are several things you can do to make your work enjoyable and productive when you start again:

◆ Try to end your work on a high note. If you quit at a point of satisfaction, you will tend to think of the work as gratifying and be more eager to return to it.

◆ Try to stop at a point of accomplishment.

◆ If you quit at a point where you are stalled, write down the problem and try to clarify what's blocking your progress.

◆ Have a logical starting point at which to resume. This will reduce your start-up time when you return to the task.

Improve Your Follow-through

Knowing when to stop is a good tactical manoeuvre, but it doesn't get the job done. Somewhere along the line you must tackle the task and follow through to completion. Here are some ideas that you will find helpful in successfully finishing what you start. Some of them have been, or will be, discussed in greater detail elsewhere in this book.

◆ Become interested in your work. Interest and motivation go hand-in-hand. Obtain as much information as you can about a task. The more you know about something, the more likely you are to become absorbed in it.

◆ Try to imagine the satisfaction that will come from completing the task. Think of how much better you will look after you've shed those excess kilograms or how much better you will feel when you quit smoking. Think of the better job you will have and the happier life you will lead when you finally get that degree or that promotion. As I write this book I imagine myself walking past a bookshop and seeing the book in the window. I imagine people telling me how it helped them to lead happier lives. I imagine all the things I'll be able to do with the royalty cheques. Do you know what? I'm really getting excited! Let's move on to the next idea so that I can finish the book.

◆ Challenge yourself with deadlines for completion.

◆ Try to shield yourself from interruptions and distractions.

◆ Take part in a joint effort with someone else who is dependable. When you make a commitment to do something with someone else, you are more likely to do the job than if you tackle it alone. When I was at university, we studied in groups or pairs to reinforce our commitment to learn. We called it 'co-operate and graduate'. The important thing is that each person be dependable. If both parties are committed, each can set the pace for the other.

Improve Your Memory

One of our greatest time- and energy-saving tools is our memory. Without a memory, all of our learning would be useless. We would have to respond to every situation as if we had never experienced it. We use our memories to learn to walk, talk, absorb facts, solve problems, drive cars, read and do numerous other things. The uses and capacity of the human memory are a miracle. Our brains can store more information than today's most advanced computers.

Unfortunately, storing information is one thing and retrieving it is another. This is where the computer is our superior. However, most of us can improve our ability to store and retrieve information if we understand how our memory works and apply some simple concepts of memory improvement.

Memory skills are generally divided into these stages:

- **Remembering** — leaving the information to be stored.
- **Recording** — storing the material in the brain until it is needed.
- **Retrieving** — getting the material out when needed. This final stage is the cause of our greatest problems. How many times have you said to yourself, 'It's on the tip of my tongue'?

We can do little or nothing to improve our retrieval ability *per se*. However, our ability to retrieve is somewhat dependent on how we record information, and so we can improve our memory by modifying our methods of recording. Here are some guidelines to help you make the most of your memory:

- Commit things to memory when you are rested. If you try to memorise when you are fatigued, you will most likely find it frustrating.
- Break lists up into smaller, manageable units and subcategories before trying to memorise them.
- Repeat the material to yourself several times. Writing the material down also helps.
- Space your learning over several periods. Begin each new period by reviewing what you have previously memorised to keep it firmly planted in your memory.

◆ Relate material you are learning to familiar ideas, persons, symbols or other things that are already firmly planted in your memory. For example, you can probably recall roughly what the map of Italy looks like, because it's shaped like a boot. Can you do the same for Chile?

◆ Arrange ideas to be learned into a formula system or code word to aid your recall. For example, sales trainers use the code word AIDA, which stands for 'arouse Attention, create Interest, stimulate Desire and move to Action'.

◆ Use spare moments, such as waiting time, for memorising. Carry note cards in your pocket for quick and easy referral.

If you use some of the modern memory aids, known an mnemonics, you will amaze yourself and others with your feats of memory. With proper training, almost anyone can learn to look through a shuffled deck of cards and remember them in order, meet 50 people and instantly recall their names, or recall over 100 phone numbers. If you want more information on memory improvement, there are several good books on the subject, including Harry Lorayne's *Page-a-Minute Memory Book*.

Deal with Trivia in Batches

All of us are plagued with minor but necessary tasks that must be carried out regularly. Examples of these are paying bills, running errands, shopping, housework, gardening, minor repairs, correspondence and making telephone calls. Attacking these tasks in a random fashion is one sure way to work more and accomplish less.

One way to keep trivia from hindering your effectiveness is to organise the tasks into batches and handle a batch at a time. Try to run several errands at one time. Go to the supermarket, bank, video store and petrol station in one trip. Do several household chores in sequence, or combine several if possible. Pay all of your bills at a certain time each month. Try to make telephone calls and to write letters in batches. Trivia sessions are an effective method of preventing the minor things in your life from hindering your accomplishment of major goals.

PROBLEM SOLVING STRATEGY

As you are aware by now, planning and goal-achieving are basically a process of decision making, and decision making is problem solving. Organising your approach to a problem puts you halfway towards solving it. The following general guidelines will help you to achieve a basic readiness to meet and penetrate all roadblocks to success.

Don't Needlessly Complicate Your Problems

We live in an age of technological sophistication, complete with virtual reality and nuclear power. Complexity is the norm. As a result, we have come to expect complexity in all facets of life. There appears to be an unwritten rule in our society that nothing has the right to be simple any more. All too often when given the choice between a simple and a complex solution to a problem, many of us opt for the latter. The joke about five people being needed to change a light bulb (one to hold the bulb and four to turn the person on the ladder) makes us chuckle. But, like most good humour, it contains an element of truth. When you are trying to solve a problem, look first for a simple, satisfactory solution. It may save you a great deal of time.

Approach the Problem Creatively

Often our problem solving ability is hindered by being locked into a particular way of viewing the problem. You might have heard the story of the truck that was stuck in an underpass. A team of engineers was called out to decide how to dislodge the truck. True to their profession, they took an engineering approach to solving the problem and began making a series of complex stress calculations. A small boy standing by the road asked one of the engineers, 'Why don't you let the air out of the tyres?' Immediately, the problem was solved.

The more ways we allow ourselves to view a problem, the better the odds of our finding a satisfactory solution.

Distinguish between Urgency and Importance

Most of us have tried to arrange our work so that we need only attend to urgent and important matters. Everything else is to be delegated to lower echelons. We soon learn, however, that urgency and importance seldom appear together. This concept also applies to our lives. Important things are seldom urgent, and urgent things are seldom important. The urgency of fixing a flat tyre when you are late for an appointment is much greater than remembering to pay your car insurance premium, but its importance is, in most cases, relatively small.

Unfortunately, many of us spend our lives fighting fires under the tyranny of the urgent. The result is that we ignore the less urgent but more important things in life. This is a great effectiveness killer.

When you are faced with a number of problems to solve, ask yourself which are the important ones and make them your first priority. If you allow yourself to be governed by the tyranny of the urgent, your life will be spent dealing with one crisis after another. You'll be very active and may even be the busiest beaver around. However, one day you may wake up to find that you've been building your dam on an empty lake.

Try to Anticipate Potential Crises

Doctors tell us that the best medicine is preventive medicine. So, take precautionary measures designed to maintain your health, such as getting enough rest, maintaining a proper diet, exercising regularly etc.

General problem solving operates in much the same way. If you anticipate crises, take steps to prevent or deal with them, you will be wisely investing your time. Things seldom evolve to the crisis level without some warning. A little foresight can ensure that you spend your time achieving your goals rather than reacting to crises.

Put Your Subconscious to Work

Some of our greatest problem solving ability lies somewhere beneath our level of awareness. Often we have trouble coming up with solutions to problems simply because we are pressing ourselves too hard for an answer. The anxiety and tension we create by agonising over a solution stifles our creative abilities and wastes time.

The more we press ourselves for an answer, the less effective our problem solving skills. The best solution is to put your subconscious to work. Turn the problem over to it. You can do this by relaxing just before you go to sleep. Visualise your problem and the result you want. The answer can often just come to you, or if that fails, try some old-fashioned advice and, 'Sleep on it'.

CHAPTER 4

MAKING EVERY DAY COUNT

*Many people assume that they can probably
find many ways to save time.
This is an incorrect assumption for it
is only when you focus on
spending time that you begin to
use your time effectively.*

MERRILL DOUGLASS

'WHERE DID THE week go? I've been working like a demon from dawn until dusk, and all I have to show for my effort is exhaustion.'

'I have so much to do that I feel overwhelmed. It's like someone just handed me a bucket and told me to go bale out Sydney Harbour.'

All of us are given the same amount of time in a given day, week or month. However, we have only to look around us to see that some of us get a great deal more mileage out of our days than others. In this chapter, we will concern ourselves with two facets of time: how to account for it, and how to schedule for the effective use of it.

HOW DO YOU SPEND YOUR TIME?

Do you really know how you spend your time? We think we do, but the truth is that most of us don't. The plain fact about our use of time is that it is mostly a matter of habit. Habits are time-savers and allow us to do things without having to stop and think. However, many habits are useless practices that needlessly dissipate our time. Since we practise these habits without much thought, it follows that we aren't aware of them unless we make a conscious effort to discover them.

It's much easier to bury our heads in the sand than to observe and account for our behaviour. Most of us would prefer not to face ourselves. To make an objective appraisal of our use of time takes a tremendous amount of courage. However, if you are willing to do it for one week, you will undoubtedly find it beneficial.

The following time inventory exercise will reveal many things about what you really do with your time. If you have the courage to recognise your bad habits, you will greatly increase the odds of reducing and eliminating them. You will be taking a giant step towards working smarter by trying to discover and reduce time-wasting behaviour.

After the inventory, we will consider some ways to make better use of your time.

**Prepare a one-week time inventory statement,
like that shown on pp 61–63.**

1. Fill in your estimated time for each activity.

2. Fill in the actual time you spend on each activity. You don't have to account for every minute; just record realistically how you spend the bulk of each half-hour for one week – not what you think you did!

3. Record the variances.

4. Complete the column showing the percentage of your total time taken up by each activity.

5. Calculate the totals for each group of activities.

6. Complete the summary statement to give you a broader picture of how you spend your time.

TIME INVENTORY
STATEMENT

	Estimated Weekly Time	Actual Weekly Time	Variance	Percentage of Weekly Time Spent
Work activities				
1. Commuting to and from work	*e.g. 8 hrs*	*9 hrs*	*+1 hrs*	*5.4%*
2. Meetings	—	—	—	—
3. Telephone calls	—	—	—	—
4. Reading	—	—	—	—
5. Paper-work and correspondence	—	—	—	—
6. Assisting colleagues	—	—	—	—
7. Delegating work	—	—	—	—
8. Troubleshooting	—	—	—	—
9. Drop-in visitors	—	—	—	—
10 Seeing the boss	—	—	—	—
11. Travelling	—	—	—	—
12. Calling on customers	—	—	—	—
13. Lunch and coffee breaks	—	—	—	—
14. Miscellaneous	—	—	—	—
SUB-TOTAL	—	—	—	—

	Estimated WEEKLY TIME	Actual WEEKLY TIME	Variance	Percentage OF WEEKLY TIME SPENT
Personal activities				
15. Grooming and Personal Care	—	—	—	—
16. Eating	—	—	—	—
17. Sleeping	—	—	—	—
18. Miscellaneous	—	—	—	—
SUB-TOTAL	—	—	—	—
Family activities				
19. Cooking	—	—	—	—
20. Housework	—	—	—	—
21. Washing clothes	—	—	—	—
22. Gardening	—	—	—	—
23. Household maintenance	—	—	—	—
24. Grocery shopping	—	—	—	—
25. Other shopping	—	—	—	—
26. Paying bills	—	—	—	—
27. Child care activities	—	—	—	—
28. Religious activities	—	—	—	—
29. Family outings	—	—	—	—
30. Family time	—	—	—	—
31. Miscellaneous	—	—	—	—
SUB-TOTAL	—	—	—	—

	Estimated Weekly Time	Actual Weekly Time	Variance	Percentage of Weekly Time Spent
LEISURE ACTIVITIES				
32. Listening to music	—	—	—	—
33. Watching TV and videos	—	—	—	—
34. Reading	—	—	—	—
35. Hobbies	—	—	—	—
36. Spectator sports and recreation	—	—	—	—
37. Participant sports	—	—	—	—
38. Travel	—	—	—	—
39. Parties and socialising	—	—	—	—
40. Miscellaneous	—	—	—	—
OTHER ACTIVITIES				
41. Miscellaneous	—	—	—	—
SUB-TOTAL	—	—	—	—
TOTAL	—	—	—	100%

TIME INVENTORY SUMMARY

	Estimated Weekly Time	Actual Weekly Time	Variance	Percentage of Weekly Time Spent
Total work activities	*e.g. 45*	50	–5	29.8%
Total personal activities	—	—	—	—
Total family activities	—	—	—	—
Total leisure activities	—	—	—	—
Total other activities	—	—	—	—
TOTAL	—	—	—	100%

Once you have completed the time inventory exercise and have become thoroughly familiar with the data, your next step is to use this information to help you make better use of your time in the future. No doubt you found some real surprises and not all of them were pleasant. The task now is to be scrupulously honest with yourself when performing the following exercise.

Take several sheets of paper, your time inventory statement and summary, and your written goals, and go somewhere where you will be alone and undisturbed.
After careful consideration, write answers to the following questions:

1. How did I waste my time? What can I do to prevent or reduce wasted time in the future?

2. How did I waste other people's time? Whose time did I waste? How can I prevent this from happening?

3. What activities am I now performing that can be reduced, eliminated or given to someone else to do?

4. What did other people do that wasted my time? Can anything be done to reduce or eliminate future occurrences? If so, what?

5. What did I do that was urgent but unimportant?

6. What did I do that was important in light of my goals?

7. Am I spending my time pursuing those things that are important to me? If not, why not? If so, how?

The answers to these questions should provide you with plenty of ideas that will enable you to make better use of your time. It's also an excellent idea to make a regular practice of taking a one-week time inventory every six months. It's much easier the second time around, as you know how to do it and there will be fewer surprises. You will probably find an improvement in your effectiveness after making a conscious effort at planning and goal-setting. New bad habits can be readily uncovered and eliminated before they become deeply ingrained. Samuel Johnson, the English lexicographer, critic and poet, once remarked, 'The chains of habits are too weak to be felt until they are too strong to be broken.' A periodic time inventory will help you to break those chains.

TIME OVER WHICH
WE HAVE NO CONTROL

Now that we know how we spend our time, the following exercise will help you to see the amount of time over which we have no control.

Draw up a weekly planner like that shown on page 66. Now black out the time taken up permanently or consistently by meetings, out-of-town trips, medical or dental appointments, recreation, travelling time, etc. There is only one criterion: if you *must* do it, you don't have control.

After completing the exercises in this chapter, you will know two important things about your time:

◆ What you do with it.
◆ How much of it you can control.

Peter Drucker, author of a number of bestselling books on work practices, says that 'the reality of our working life is that others move in on us and use up our time' and that 'one of our major responsibilities is to make others effective'.

We know from experience that this is true. Our bosses, colleagues and subordinates all demand, and must get, part of our time. The key is to restrict it to what is *necessary*. Even if we manage to do only what is necessary, we will, after allowing for time over which we have no control, be lucky to have 15 to 20 hours a week at our absolute disposal. During this time, we must accomplish those key tasks which will largely decide the degree of success we enjoy. Thus, priorities and planning will always be the main concern of those who want to rise above the ordinary.

WEEKLY PLANNER

Time	Sun	Mon	Tues	Wed	Thurs	Fri	Sat
Morning							
8.30							
9.00							
9.30							
10.00							
10.30							
11.00							
11.30							
12.00							
12.30							
1.00							
1.30							
2.00							
2.30							
3.00							
3.30							
4.00							
4.30							
5.00							
5.30							
Evening							

#1 GOAL _____ WEEK OF_____

REPLACING OLD HABITS WITH NEW ONES

Somerset Maugham, the English writer, once said, 'The unfortunate thing about this world is that good habits are so much easier to give up than bad ones.' He might also have mentioned that it is easier to cling to old habits than it is to adopt new ones. Inertia makes change difficult. Turning the momentum in favour of new habits is not impossible, but it *is* difficult. What it requires can be summed up in two words: will power.

Almost a century ago, William James wrote a scientific paper on how to develop good habits and break bad ones. Time has not diminished the value of what James had to say. He listed three key points to follow in replacing old habits with new ones.

First, launch the new habit with strength and commitment. Devise a new routine to contrast with the old. Tell your friends or announce the change publicly. If you decide to lose a few kilograms this month, tell your family and friends that you plan to do so and how you plan to do it. This will build up your momentum and quell any cravings for between-meal snacks. Every time you feel like going to the refrigerator, you will think of all the people you made a commitment to.

James's second recommendation was to practise the new habit without exception until it is firmly rooted. Any lapse in practising the new habit only gives momentum back to the old one. It's much like having to start all over, and getting started is the hardest part.

Finally, James recommended that we put our new habits into use at the earliest possible opportunity. Waiting until next month to start getting up an hour earlier, or to save for a new house, or to stop smoking only increases the odds that it will never get done. Good habits are acquired and strengthened by practice, not by procrastination. One great tip to overcoming time-wasting habits is to acquire the habit of scheduling. Without further delay, let's look at some ideas that will enable you to work less and accomplish more through effective scheduling.

KEYS TO EFFECTIVE SCHEDULING

Like all other planning, effective scheduling is best done on paper. A good scheduling tool to use is a weekly planner, like the one we used for the last exercise. This enables you to see an entire week at a glance, which will help you to schedule how it should be used. It also provides a place for listing a top goal that you wish to achieve during the week.

What type of schedule form you use is a personal choice. What matters most is that you use one that is suited to your lifestyle and tastes. Some of us schedule quite effectively with a simple desk calendar. Others prefer a large monthly wall calendar with ample writing space by each date. Some people like to use a combination of schedules — one monthly, one weekly and one daily. Choose a style that you feel comfortable with. Being overly organised is no virtue, and when carried to extremes can be as bad as total chaos.

Block Out Planning Time

Be sure to set aside a period of each day for thinking, reflecting and planning. This quiet time will help you to organise your thoughts about where you are going and how today will help you get there. For most of us, this is best accomplished as the first item of the day. For others, it is best scheduled in the evening or as the last item on the workday agenda.

Whatever time of day you set aside for planning, just be sure you do it. It will repay you many times over. Never tell yourself that you are too busy to plan. Probably one of the reasons you're so busy is that you didn't take the time to plan. You've created a vicious circle for yourself. It's much like the proverb, 'He who rides a tiger can never dismount'. To make planning effective, set aside time in blocks of at least half an hour. Planning time is thinking time. It is high-priority time, so give it the time it deserves. If you can only spare five or 10 minutes, then start preparing for your planning session by getting what you need ready.

Put Important Deadlines on Your Schedule

In Chapter 2, I pointed out that a goal should have a deadline. Deadlines aid the scheduling process when handled in the following manner:

- ◆ Determine the deadline target date and mark it on your schedule.
- ◆ Estimate the amount of time you will need to complete the task at hand. Remember Murphy's Law: everything will take longer than you expect.

◆ Once you have estimated how much time a task will consume, work back from the deadline and block off some remaining hours to devote to the task. This will also tell you the latest possible date you can expect to start the task and successfully meet the deadline.

Design a Flexible Schedule

Life is — and always will be — full of surprises. We can always expect the unexpected to come along and disrupt the best of plans. The only way to deal with the unexpected is to budget time for it. Failure to give ourselves breathing room in scheduling is where most of us make our greatest scheduling error. If we insist on running on a tight schedule, we are inviting the unexpected to raise havoc and destroy our scheduling efforts. Besides, tight schedules aren't much fun.

In scheduling, I have found this rule of thumb works for me: estimate how much time you think a given activity or task will take and multiply it by 1.25. Thus, if I think a dental appointment will take an hour, I allow an hour and 15 minutes in my schedule. If I think it will take four hours to prepare a lecture, I schedule five. If the task is something I'm totally unfamiliar with or have never done before, I estimate the time and multiply it by 1.5. Another excellent rule of thumb is to schedule only 50 per cent of your time.

Block Out Time for Recreation and Diversion

It is bizarre that a recommendation for blocking out time for relaxation and recreation has to be made. Yet we have only to look around us to see how many people cease to function fully when away from the job. Workaholics are usually very ambitious individuals who are willing to pay any price to get to the top. Unfortunately, what many of them fail to realise is that their compulsion to work can hinder their job effectiveness. By not taking time to get away from it all, compulsive workers lose the long-range perspective necessary for real success. They fail to see the forest for the trees.

The more stressful the work, the greater the need for frequent diversion or recreation. If you look at the total picture of highly successful people, you will generally find a great deal more to their lives than their jobs. They may live to work, but they also live for a great deal more.

Make it a point to rediscover your non-vocational self and block out time to do so. Develop some outside interests or hobbies. It doesn't really matter what they are, as long as you enjoy them and they allow you to escape mentally and/or physically. For some this may be tennis, while for others it may be collecting old porcelain.

You will also find that your effectiveness will be improved if you allow for breaks during your workday. What is best in terms of the number and length of breaks depends on the type of work and you.

To get the most from your breaks, experiment with various systems until you find one that harmoniously combines comfort and results. The important thing to remember is that diversion is necessary for increased effectiveness as well as enjoyment.

AVOID OVERCOMMITMENT — LEARN TO SAY NO

The artist James Whistler believed that the secret to successful painting was knowing what *not* to put on canvas. Similarly, your success at working smart depends on knowing what *not* to do. Master the ability of knowing how and when to say no, and half the battle is won.

Overcommitment is one of the most frequent ways we dilute our effectiveness. As I pointed out in Chapter 1, devoting a little of yourself to everything means you aren't able to commit a great deal of yourself to anything. You are left unable to concentrate on the important goals with the highest payoffs. Unfortunately, many of us just don't know how to refuse a request for our time when we could be putting it to better use. We usually say yes for two reasons: we are afraid someone else will have a lesser opinion of us; or a request for our help indulges our ego by giving us a feeling of power.

Don't misunderstand me — I'm not against helping people. What I'm referring to are the times we say yes when we know it's in our best interests to say no. When you say yes because of a need for approval, you are in effect saying to yourself that someone else's opinion of you is more important than your opinion of yourself. Saying yes to indulge your ego is the ammunition of martyrs. The hidden message is 'You owe it all to me', with the emphasis on *owe*. It's a covert way of obligating others.

Make it a point to politely and directly refuse requests that are not in your own best interests. Learning to say no is like learning to swim. You increase your proficiency with practice.

Getting to No

The following guidelines will help you to improve your ability to say no. The proper application of this most negative word can have very positive consequences in helping you to manage your time effectively.

◆ Offer your refusals politely and pleasantly. There's no need to be defensive — it's okay to say no.

◆ Say no before people can anticipate that you may say yes. Answers such as 'I don't know' or 'Let me think about it' only get people's hopes up. A delayed refusal only increases the chances of animosity.

◆ Realise that you have the right to say no. You don't have to offer a reason every time you turn down someone's request.

◆ Offer a counter-proposal if you think it's appropriate and the request is a valid one. Such an approach softens your refusal.

If knowing what *not* to do is such an important aspect of working smart, it seems only fitting that we should have a not-to-do list. There's no need to sit down each day and make such a list. Rather, I have compiled a general list of things which are better left undone.

Not-to-do List

◆ All low-priority items — unless the high-priority items have been completed.

◆ Any task whose completion is of little or no consequence. When you have something to do, ask yourself the worst thing that could happen if you don't do it. If the answer isn't too bad, then don't do it.

◆ Anything that you can give to someone else to do.

◆ Anything just to please others because you fear their condemnation or you want to put them in your debt.

◆ Thoughtless or inappropriate requests for your time and effort.

◆ Anything others should be doing for themselves.

When you find yourself working hard and accomplishing little, remember the not-to-do list. It may help you to define the problem.

MAKE THE MOST OF PRIME TIME

Prime time is the time of day when you are at your best in performing a given task. You will find that you can accomplish more with less effort if you schedule important tasks at the time of day when you perform them best.

Just what is prime time depends upon the person and the job. If you have a task requiring solitude and concentration, schedule it for the time of day at which you concentrate best. For many of us, this is before 9 a.m., whereas others may concentrate best late in the evening. If the task involves others, try to avoid scheduling in the morning if you are a less-than-sociable morning person. I have one close friend who is barely a functioning human being before 3 p.m. He seems to be at his best between 10 p.m. and 2 a.m. Fortunately he has a career in broadcasting that enables him to take advantage of late-night prime time.

LOOK FOR WAYS TO CAPITALISE ON COMMITTED TIME

In scheduling a given day, you will block out time for certain essentials such as showering, dressing, and commuting to and from work. However, sometimes you can put committed time to a second use. For example, a friend of mine, who is working towards a Master of Business Administration degree, studies while showering, dressing and driving to work. He does this by first recording his class notes on a cassette tape recorder and then playing them back in the morning. Another friend, a sales representative, uses commuting time to memorise the names of his customers and salient details about each individual. He also uses a cassette recorder.

Another type of committed time we can put to further use is waiting time. Most of us simply write off the time we spend waiting for the doctor, the dentist or the hair stylist. However, with a little effort we can squeeze all sorts of activities into these minutes. While waiting for an appointment, you can plan your weekend, update your goals or your daily to-do list, do isometric exercises, pay bills, meditate, write letters, or you can simply use this time to relax.

Also, there are plenty of major projects that you can nibble away at during occasional spare moments. You could work on your Italian vocabulary exercises, plan your dream home or outline the detective novel you've always wanted to write. With a little imagination, you can easily come up with plenty of ideas.

Another type of committed time is shopping time. Going to the supermarket or shopping centre can consume huge amounts of time, most of which is unproductive. The best way to make effective use of shopping time is to minimise it, and this means shopping during periods of least activity. Avoid supermarkets and shopping centres on weekends. Arrange your schedule so that you shop weekdays or in the evenings. Do your banking in the morning and avoid the lunch-hour crowd. Better yet, take advantage of telephone banking. If you find yourself stuck in a queue, be prepared to have something to do. Carry a memory list and resolve to memorise such things as frequently called telephone numbers, or names and important facts about customers.

Another good way to capitalise on committed time is to carry a notebook, a dictation recorder or an electronic organiser for jotting down ideas that come to mind. Mobile phones also enable you to catch up on calls during otherwise unproductive interludes.

Most of us view time from the perspective of hours, days and weeks. It's the minutes and our overall life span that we seem most apt to ignore. With a little thought, we can make the most of both.

A FINAL THOUGHT ON SCHEDULING

While you were reading the suggestions on scheduling contained in this chapter, you may have thought, 'I can't *always* do that.' Rest assured, none of us can. Life is far from perfect. On many occasions, you may not be able to make your schedule as flexible as you would like. Unfortunately, the nature of your job may not permit you to use the prime-time concept to your greatest advantage. None of us are able to apply all of these ideas all of the time — and wouldn't life be dull if we could!

The point is that all of us can apply all of these concepts *some* of the time. The more we are alert to and apply these ideas, the more we will be able to accomplish with a given amount of time and effort. And that's what working smarter is all about.

CHAPTER 5

NEW ATTITUDES FOR EFFECTIVENESS

*One sees great things from the valley;
only small things from the peak.*

G. K. CHESTERTON

LIFE IS AN attitude, and work is a large part of our lives. How we spend our time and energy is also a matter of attitude. Tell me what you think and how you feel and I'll tell you who you are. How hard we work and how much or little we accomplish is largely governed by our thoughts and feelings.

In the process of going through life, we gather beliefs about our thoughts and feelings and, like the work tapes, many of these beliefs are false. We have been programmed to believe that our feelings are something mysterious, uncontrollable and independent of our thoughts. The notion that 'really living' means a life of highly uncontrollable emotional experiences is another concept we are bombarded with. We are taught to be responsible for the feelings and attitudes of others. We learn that the 'conscientious, good person' is someone who feels guilty about their past and worries about their future and the future of others. It's a wonder that *anything* gets accomplished with the massive amount of time and energy that is wasted each day on sustaining these myths.

YOU'RE BETTER THAN YOU THINK YOU ARE!

When it comes to self-evaluation, we tend to sell ourselves short. We are smarter, stronger, more creative and more talented than we believe we are. Most of us never come anywhere near tapping the reservoir of potential within us. Why this is, I cannot say for sure; but in my opinion our greatest limiting factor is our concept of who we are — our self-image.

If we want to improve our performance, we must first improve our self-image. If there is no change in self-image, there can be no change in performance, because it is impossible for us to consistently outperform our current self-image.

Over the years, I have observed that coaches in all kinds of sports operate from the assumption that we are all better than we believe we are. Their main role is to change those self-limiting beliefs.

It appears that our self-image is at the core of all our behaviour and its preservation is a motive for practically everything we do. We cling tenaciously to any ideas we have about ourselves, for better or for worse. What this does is create a self-fulfilling prophecy in which our behaviour confirms our self-image. If you believe that you are shy, aggressive, worthwhile, friendly or intelligent, your behaviour will tend to support your concept of who you are.

We cling to self-concepts and resist changes in them because they are our main contact with reality. To lose contact with oneself is indeed traumatic. Yet many things we believe about our inherent makeup are simply untrue or are rationalisations. How many times have you heard someone say, 'I'm sorry, but that's just the way I am'? People's strongest motivation is not self-preservation but preservation of their self-image.

Strengthening your self-image is a key to increased effectiveness. In the final analysis, winners above all see themselves as winners. They may not win them all, but they sure win more than their share. Unfortunately, the self-fulfilling prophecy holds equally true for losers.

Strengthen Your Self-image

A stronger self-image gives us the 'can do' power to climb to the highest summits and have energy to spare. Changing your self-image is tough, but it can be done with a little will power and self-discipline. The following guidelines will help you to bolster your self-worth.

PUT THE PAST IN THE PAST

In the process of maturing, we all encounter experiences that contribute to the formation of our self-image. Unfortunately, we are left clinging to erroneous ideas about our abilities and character traits. Those ideas that affect our work are such self-defeating statements as:

- I lack initiative.
- I don't express myself well.
- I can't handle responsibility.
- I'm not assertive.
- I'm not strong.
- I can't think clearly.
- I have to work twice as hard as most people.
- I rebel against authority.
- I'm lazy.
- I'm disorganised and undisciplined.
- I'll go crazy if I don't keep busy.
- I can't work without supervision.
- I'm not a good worker.
- I'm unworthy of an important position or promotion.
- I'm sarcastic and abrasive.

Many of the things we tell ourselves about ourselves are true only because we choose to believe they are. Or we behaved in an unsatisfactory manner in the past because we believed we were that way.

This trap can be beaten by putting the past in proper perspective. Yesterday is further away than the last day of your life, because yesterday will never come again.

Instead of saying, 'I'm unorganised' or 'I lack initiative', say 'I've chosen to be that way in the past, but today is another story.' Then write yourself some goals designed to contradict those statements. If you've been telling yourself you lack initiative, start a new task or project that will increase your value to the company. Make a list of all the 'I am's' you believe about yourself, and then write a plan of action for proving yourself wrong. Follow through on your plans and you will soon have a lot of weight taken off your shoulders as the ghosts of the past vanish.

BUILD ON YOUR STRENGTHS

Everyone's self-image is a mixture of both positive and negative qualities. Thus, in addition to rectifying negatives, you can enhance your self-image by dwelling on your present positive qualities and using them to best advantage.

Make a list of your positive traits and include examples that prove you have these qualities. For instance, if you think you're good with interpersonal relationships, note the time you landed the company that important contract through your own personal charm, or the time you resolved a misunderstanding that prevented a valuable employee from resigning.

After you have listed your strengths, consider them in light of your goals. How can you use them to help you achieve your goals? Which ones will be most useful in this regard?

If you stop and take stock of your strengths, you will be amazed at how many good traits you have. Don't be modest and hold back. Build yourself up! Then resolve to make the most of your strengths. It's the psychological leverage of working smart.

ACCEPT YOURSELF — UNCONDITIONALLY

Never confuse your intrinsic worth with your external successes, failures, triumphs or tragedies. You are a perfectly valuable, worthwhile individual simply because you exist. It's okay to be you.

Conditionally accepting yourself is one way to ensure that you will never be totally at peace with yourself. How many times have you thought, 'I'll be worthwhile when I graduate from university, get a driver's licence, make $50 000 a year, own my own home, get promoted, pay off the mortgage, get a raise . . .' and so on? Yet no sooner do we reach one goal than there is another 'I'll be okay when . . .' beckoning to us. You're okay *now*.

DON'T ALLOW OTHERS TO DEFINE YOUR WORTH

Building your self-image on others' opinions of you is like building the foundation of a house on a bed of quicksand. Sooner or later it's bound to cave in. Unfortunately, we are taught from the cradle to the grave that behaviour that results in the approval of others is the key to our happiness and well-being. Society sends out all sorts of messages, some subtle and others not so subtle, about what should be important to us and how we should behave. Practically all advertising is based on the value of pleasing others. Over and over, the message is: 'Buy the product and be accepted, loved, esteemed and more worthwhile.' We are all happier when we enjoy the approval of others. However, we have magnified its importance so much that many of us tie it to our self-image.

By and large, people are fickle, and the one that loves and praises you today may not do so tomorrow. Whenever someone rejects, condemns or tries to belittle you, remember what Eleanor Roosevelt, the former American First Lady, said: 'No one can make you feel inferior without your consent.'

It is also wise to refrain from letting others define your capabilities. Never let anyone tell you you're too old, too young, too lazy or too anything to accomplish what you want. If it seems possible to you and you want to do it, then move full-speed ahead. As the American philosopher Ralph Waldo Emerson wrote, 'Self trust is the first secret of success.'

Our world has experts on every corner telling people what they are and aren't capable of. And for every expert, there are at least a hundred people proving them wrong.

PUT WHAT YOU WANT FIRST

For years, we have been fed another social message, and that is to subordinate our desires to those of others in order to achieve a better world. So we sacrifice our own needs for the good of our spouse, children, company or government.

The problem with such a philosophy is that it ultimately breeds resentment on the part of all concerned. You don't help the poor by becoming one of them. You help them by keeping your own needs satisfied and helping them to help themselves.

Much the same is true for all of our other relationships. Positive selfishness is the prerequisite to forming good relationships with others. Until you feel good and self-satisfied about your own life, you have little to offer someone else to help theirs.

To quote from the Talmud: 'Every man has the right to feel "because of me the world was created".' If you are burning with altruistic desires, I would suggest you adopt that viewpoint. You can't fill an empty bucket with a dry well. It's much as George Bernard Shaw, the playwright, said: 'A man's interest in the world is only the overflow of his interest in himself.'

Only You Control Your Thoughts and Feelings

Developing effective work attitudes begins with understanding your feelings and where they come from. Contrary to popular belief, your feelings are not a mystical, uncontrollable phenomenon that governs your behaviour. How many times have you heard someone tell another to 'stop feeling and start thinking' or something to that effect? In reality, this is an absurd statement because without thinking there is no feeling.

Only after you think about something do you choose how you will feel. For example, you're at work and someone tells you that the boss is very displeased with your performance and wants to see you this afternoon. Upon hearing this, you may feel guilty, worried or apathetic, or you may choose to forget it until you talk with the boss. The point is that until you got the message and had time to think about it, it was impossible for you to have any feelings concerning the matter.

Most of us don't believe that we can control our feelings, but we know that with a little self-discipline we can control our thoughts. However, if we can control our thoughts, and feelings come from thoughts, then it follows logically that we can control our feelings.

An example of feelings are the attitudes we have towards the days of the week. Most of us feel a certain way on Mondays, another way on Fridays and so on. However, how would you know how to feel on Monday if you didn't know it was Monday? The simple fact is you wouldn't. Each Monday, you wake up, think to yourself 'It's Monday' and then make a decision on how to feel about it.

If we control our feelings, we choose to be happy, sad, guilty, worried, anxious or enthusiastic. Nobody makes us happy. We make ourselves happy, and the same holds true for the other emotions we experience. Don't expect anyone to make you happy, enthusiastic, motivated or energetic about your work. That's your decision.

You may feel that being responsible for your own feelings seems rather awesome; in fact, such a philosophy takes a lot of pressure off you. If you accept the premise that people must satisfy themselves, then you aren't responsible for anyone's happiness but your own. Emerson put it nicely: 'Most of the shadows of this life are caused by standing in one's own sunshine.' With that thought in mind, let's take a look at some of the shadows that result in fatigue and frustration.

GUILT — A BAD CASE OF THE 'SHOULD HAVES'

Of all the effectiveness-killing emotions, guilt is absolutely the most useless. No amount of regret, remorse or bad feeling can change the past. However, guilt, by definition, is feeling bad and becoming immobile over that which has occurred or should have occurred earlier. You can rewrite history, but you can't relive it.

If guilt is such a futile, irrational waster of time and energy, then why do we spend so much of our life being consumed by it? There are several answers.

First and foremost is the fact that we were fed large doses of guilt conditioning as children. Parents, teachers and religious institutions sometimes use guilt to regulate behaviour. As children we were taught what behaviour was right and wrong. Then we were told that our role was to feel good when we were right and bad when we were wrong. Such behaviour and thinking are carried over into adulthood. As a result, we see guilt used in some form to regulate behaviour in practically every institution and area of society.

However, there are several other reasons why we may choose to spend our efforts on guilt. Guilt is a tremendous cop-out for not being effective. If you're busy feeling guilty, you don't have to use the present to get something done.

Guilt gives you a perfect excuse for not changing yourself. You do something that isn't self-enhancing, 'pay your dues' by feeling bad about it, and life goes on. You avoid the risks as well as the work that go with positive self-improvement. It's another application of the easy-way tape.

Guilt is a great way to hold others responsible for your behaviour and your feelings, thus exonerating yourself from any wrongdoing. Such behaviour often manifests itself in statements such as 'See what they made me do', 'If it weren't for them' and 'Shame on you'.

Finally, guilt is a good way of winning the approval and pity of others. By feeling guilty, you show the world what a wonderful, conscientious, caring person you are. Unfortunately, many of us would rather be pitied than fulfilled.

When applied to work, guilt usually results in what I call a case of the 'should haves'. Symptoms of this malady can be seen in such statements as 'I should have gotten approval before taking action', 'I should have started that project earlier' and 'I should have done everything on my to-do list'. The fact is that you can't 'should have' anything. The past is history. You can only learn from it and resolve to behave differently in the present and the future.

Many of us waste a great deal of our time and energy feeling guilty about what doesn't get done. A young executive once asked me how to get more done and I recommended a to-do list to her. I bumped into her several weeks later and asked how it was working out. She replied, 'Oh, it really helped, but I had to give it up. I never got to finish the list and felt so bad that I went home each night with a headache.' Upon hearing this, I explained that she shouldn't expect to complete the list and then told her about the 80/20 rule.

'Oh! That's much better,' she replied. 'Why didn't you tell me this before?'

'I don't know,' I said. 'I guess I should have.'

Guilt over what doesn't get done gives you a lifelong ticket to misery, because you will never get everything done. Expecting to get everything done is as futile as a dog chasing its tail. However, there is always enough time to do the important things. This prayer puts everything in the proper perspective: 'Lord, there's never enough time for everything. Help me to do a little less a little better.'

Needless to say, guilt is one emotion we are better off without. The following are common-sense recommendations aimed at eliminating, or at least minimising, the pangs of guilt:

◆ Recognise the past for what it is. Write down 10 things you have done that you wish you hadn't. Then write down 10 things you didn't do that you wish you had. Give yourself five points for each item that feeling bad about will help. Your score? Zero!

◆ Practise feeling guilty. Set aside 15 or 20 minutes and think of a past event to feel bad about. Now, get in there and feel guilty! Isn't it awful! If only I hadn't! That's what I should have done! Soon you will realise what an enormous drain on your energy guilt is.

◆ List all the things you are avoiding doing by feeling guilty and resolve to do something about them. You can avoid accomplishing anything in life by feeling guilty about being lazy or lacking direction. Resolve to set your goals and spend your time achieving them rather than feeling guilty.

- ◆ Accept your past mistakes and misfortunes and resolve to learn something from them. You have the right to be wrong occasionally.
- ◆ Put the guilt wielders in their place. The world is filled with neurotic people who make it a practice to try to cast off their bad feelings on others. You need guilt wielders like you need the plague or four years of bad crops. Your only responsibility is to ignore these people or, better yet, get them out of your life.

In addition to guilt, there is another totally useless emotion that bears a strong resemblance to guilt. That emotion is . . .

WORRY

Instead of fretting and feeling guilty about the past, worriers think about all the terrible things that the future might hold. Guilt is past-oriented and worry is future-oriented. Both ensure that absolutely nothing worthwhile will be achieved in the present.

About worry, the American writer Mark Twain once remarked, 'I've suffered a great many catastrophes in my life. Most of them never happened.' The fact is that all our worries are fantasies. None of the things we worry about exist in the present and the vast majority will not exist in the future. Whatever does come to pass will certainly not be changed by worrying.

The psychological payoffs for worry are similar to those for guilt. Worrying is a great excuse for not being effective. How often have you heard someone say, 'I'm just too upset and worried to concentrate on my job'? Robert Lee Frost, the American poet, once said, 'The reason worry kills more people than work is that more people worry than work.' Worry is work, hard work — and totally unproductive at that.

Worry also shows everyone how much you care and how responsible you are. After all, it shows you're thinking about the future and not wasting time enjoying today.

Worrying is easier than changing. Instead of trying to build a better future by taking action, you can simply worry about what might happen.

Worry has one other payoff — it can get you loads of sympathy and pity. Professional worriers don't worry for nothing. They have all sorts of things to show for their efforts, like headaches, ulcers, backaches, and various other real and imagined illnesses. Pity the poor worrier — and your pity is probably just what they want.

Worrying is something all of us could do less of, because any amount is too much. Here are some things you can do to help you stop worrying:

◆ Think back to a particular time in your life, be it one, five, 10 or 20 years ago. What things did you worry about then? How many of them never came to pass? Most of them. How many did you prevent by worrying? None. How many actually happened but turned out to be blessings in disguise?

◆ Almost all of us know someone who worried excessively about their job security, and who lost their job only to find a much better position, which was better paid, in which they were much happier, and which they believe is much more challenging and interesting. Remember, you cannot discover new oceans unless you have the courage to leave the shore.

◆ Make a list of the worst things that have ever happened to you. Then ask yourself how many of them came as a total shock. Most of the real tragedies of this life are unanticipated, and what a blessing that is. You don't have a chance to worry about them beforehand, and worry wouldn't prevent their occurrence anyway.

◆ When you are worried about something, confront it. Ask yourself, 'What's the worst that could come from this?' The answer can often puts things back in to perspective. Ask yourself, 'Can I do anything about this particular problem?' If the answer is no, forget it; you can't do anything to solve it and all the worry in the world won't help. If the answer is yes, then do what you can immediately. Action is a great tension reliever, so act now and your problem will be either fully or partially resolved, and you will feel in charge and can stop worrying.

◆ Think of all the bad things that could happen to you in the next 24 hours. For example, you could die, become permanently disabled, lose a loved one or your house could burn down. You will soon realise that the list could go on forever and that you simply don't have enough time to worry about it all. So why worry about anything?

◆ Replace worrying with planning. If you're so concerned about the future, then spend your time and energy making it better. Set yourself some goals and go after them, starting now! You'll have so much fun getting absorbed in pursuing them that you won't have the time or energy for worrying. Remember that your future is being made today by the actions you take today.

By eliminating guilt and worry, you rid yourself of two major effectiveness-killing emotions. However, there are two other dragons remaining to be slain. It seems that guilt and worry have teamed up to produce a third monster, which is . . .

FEAR OF FAILURE

Stop for a moment and think of all the wonderful things in this world that never happened because someone feared failure and hadn't the courage to act. Think of all the books, songs and plays that were never written. Think of all the singers, musicians, painters and sculptors who never developed their talent because they were afraid that someone would laugh. Think of all the great labour-saving inventions and medical cures that were never developed because someone was afraid to pursue a far-out theory. And, think of all the beautiful relationships that never blossomed because one or both parties feared rejection.

The startling fact is that there is no such thing as failure. 'Failure' is merely an opinion that a given act wasn't done satisfactorily.

Like the other immobilising emotions, choosing to be governed by the fear of failure does have some short-term payoffs. Being ruled by fear of failure lets you take the easy way out. Rather than accepting the challenge of pursuing a goal, you can scratch it off your list and tell yourself that it is impossible or not worthwhile.

Reacting to a fear of failure also provides a false sense of safety and security. You can't lose a race you don't enter. Thus by not doing something, you are spared the humiliation of failure. You'll never be a winner, but you'll never be a failure either.

If you've ever met with less than success in the past (and who hasn't), the fear of failure gives you a perfect excuse for not attempting anything new. After all, what's the point in going to all that trouble for nothing?

By not trying, you give yourself the luxury of becoming a critic. You can put your time and effort into being a spectator and ridiculing all those fools who are out there trying to succeed. The most vociferous critics are generally people who are ruled by their own fear of failure.

Those who give into their fears overlook one major point. Failure is not a measure of success. And, sitting on the fence does not get you anywhere. In life, it isn't what you lose that counts, it's what you gain and what you have left.

If you find yourself immobilised due to fear of failure, here are some ideas to help you overcome it:

◆ Set your own standards of success. Remember that failure is arbitrary. Don't allow your life to be ruled by standards other than your own. You don't have to be president of the company because your father was or your spouse wants you to be. It's your choice, not theirs.

◆ Don't fall into the trap of success–failure thinking. If you set a goal and pursue it, evaluate your own performance in terms of degrees of success.

◆ Don't feel you have to succeed or achieve excellence in everything you do. There's nothing wrong with a mediocre round of golf (at least, that's what I keep telling myself) or a poor set of tennis, as long as you're having fun.

◆ Meet your fear of failure head-on. Find something you would like to do but fear failure in, and do it. Even if you don't succeed to the degree you hope to, you won't have any regrets. After all, you will be doing what you want to do. It's better to feel sorry for the things you've done than to regret missed opportunities. All ventures involve risk, but not to venture is to waste your life. As I said earlier, life is a self-fulfilling prophecy. If you never try you can't win; if you do, you might.

◆ If you do feel you have failed, recognise it as a learning experience that will make you wiser and contribute to later successes. Astute young politicians practise this. They join a political campaign fully realising they have no chance of winning. However, by throwing their hat in the ring, they get public exposure and learn the ropes of campaigning. All of the exposure and learning can some day contribute to a victorious campaign. We can learn a great deal more from our failures than our successes, provided we avail ourselves of the opportunity. If children gave up trying to walk when they first fell, the human race would still be on all fours. They succeed because they don't know about failure until we teach them.

◆ Realise that meaningful success is rarely easy and is usually preceded by a struggle. However, it's those who have the will to see it through that make it. Most of us throw in the towel too soon, when hanging in there a little longer would do the job.

ANGER

Last but not least, anger is one of the major time- and energy-killers. If anything good comes from anger and its by-products, hatred and bitterness, I've yet to see it. It accomplishes nothing, regardless of whether it's aimed at others, oneself or inanimate objects. In the final analysis, the angry person is saying, 'The world and its people must live up to my expectations.' Of course, such a demand is totally ridiculous. Anger starts wars, and unless we learn to control our anger, it may lead to the total extinction of humanity.

Like the other three immobilising emotions — guilt, worry and fear of failure — anger has its neurotic rewards. If you're angry at other things or people, then it's all their fault for not living up to your expectations. Therefore, you don't have to change.

Anger can get you loads of sympathy, attention and power over those who will allow you to manipulate them. 'Poor Geoffrey, he has such a terrible temper. It's really a shame, because he has such bad headaches, backaches and high blood pressure as a result. Let's just do what he wants. God forbid what might happen if he gets mad! And besides, it's not his fault that he's such a sensitive, intense and totally alive person.'

Anger gives you licence to go temporarily insane, thus exonerating you from responsibility for unsatisfactory behaviour. You can tell yourself and others, 'I don't know what came over me. I just lost my temper.'

Finally, anger is an excuse for incompetence. You can blame your bad temper for your inability to think straight or take constructive action.

Of course, all of these payoffs are a total waste of time and energy. Getting out of your car and kicking the tyres when you break down on the expressway isn't going to get you moving again. However, the most self-destructive anger is that which is aimed at other people. Remember: Bitterness takes too much energy and accomplishes nothing. It doesn't hurt the other person. You think you're sending out the rays of bitterness like laser beams, but they stay inside of you, consuming you.

We live in an angry age typified by high crime rates, petty bickering, broken homes and people suing each other at the drop of a hat. Whatever the reasons, there are lots of us who evidently feel that the solution to our problems is anger.

You are best off if you can eliminate your anger completely. If you can't eliminate anger, here are some useful ideas for coping with it:

◆ Vent you anger constructively. It isn't healthy to suppress anger, but there are constructive alternatives to venting it. For example, you can work out your frustrations with a regular exercise program.

◆ Sometimes a little anger can provide an additional spark to move you towards meeting your goals. I am sure you can remember when someone has been critical of your chances of succeeding in something you intended to do and their scepticism made you doubly determined to accomplish your goal. Their negative reaction got you moving. How can you thank them enough?

◆ Take your work seriously, but not yourself. Ethel Barrymore, the great entertainer, put it best when she said, 'You grow up the day you have your first real laugh at yourself.' There is absolutely no future in taking life too seriously.

◆ Develop your sense of humour and use it frequently. It is impossible to laugh and be angry at the same time. A good sense of humour creates positive energy and prevents negative emotions from clouding your life. So laugh, and enjoy your life to the hilt.

◆ Accept the fact that many things in life will not live up to your expectations. This is hardly a perfect world, and I don't know about you, but I'd feel terribly out of place if it were. Practise accepting those things in life you cannot change. Tolerance and serenity are great antidotes to anger.

◆ Give your anger a rain check. If something bothers you, count to 10 or, better yet, tell yourself, 'I'll get mad about this tomorrow.' Postponing anger is a good way to minimise it. Spontaneously unloading your anger on your boss, spouse or associates can escalate minor mishaps into major catastrophes. Postponing your anger can reduce the odds of that happening.

◆ Realise that you don't have to get mad to take constructive action. Positive, enthusiastic emotions achieve fulfilment, making good use of time and creating energy rather than draining it.

Ridding yourself of guilt, worry, fear of failure and anger can make you a new person. Suddenly you will find you have time, energy and abilities you never dreamed you had. Picture yourself as a container, and your time and energy as liquid in the container. The negative emotions are holes in the bottom of the container. To the extent that you are able to plug up the holes, you will have more time and energy to do the things in life that you find fulfilling. To carry the analogy a step further, the greater the pressure that is applied to the liquid, the faster it will drain out of the holes. This is also true with work. Best use is made of time and energy by taking the pressure off. However, before we can take the pressure off, we have to know where it is really coming from.

EASING UP THE PRESSURE

In transactional analysis, mention is made of the harried worker. He (or she) may be an executive, a clerk, a teacher, doctor, farmer or whatever. No matter what the job is, the situation is the same. A harried worker is under the gun. He is constantly overworked and complains of having to do his job and everyone else's. He takes work home in the evenings and on weekends. At work he is in constant motion and is very brief with his associates, bosses and subordinates. He says yes to all requests for his time and energy, and may even brag about not having had a holiday in 15 years. To him, hard work and life are one, and he wears his hard-work image on his shirtsleeve as a merit badge for all to admire.

Sooner or later the pressures of living the harried life begin to take their toll and the harried hero begins to deteriorate. He still says yes to all requests, but he's no longer able to come through. His appearance becomes haggard, and his eyes are bloodshot with deep circles underneath. He becomes ill and depressed. Often the final chapter of the harried worker's life is an abrupt and unexpected one. It's very common to find a harried player slumped over his desk, dead of a heart attack and surrounded by his work. The pressures of his job were just too much for him. Right? Wrong!

The harried player, like everyone else, creates his (or her) own pressure. In the final analysis, pressure — like happiness, anger, guilt, worry and fear — is internal. It's only when you choose to accept pressure that you have it. Everyone talks of hard work and the pressures of modern living, but the fact is that when we are talking about pressure we are talking about what we do to ourselves.

Virtually every chapter of this book contains advice on reducing the pressure of work. The following ideas may help to change your attitude towards work.

Approach Your Work Relaxed

When I started playing golf, I read a book to learn the fundamentals. It turned out to be an education in much more than golf. The instructions on how to swing a golf club left me with numerous things to think about every time I approached the ball. I had to think about my stance, my grip, my back swing, my hips, my follow-through, my head and so on. But the most important thing the author said to do was to relax. He was right. If you concentrate too much on every detail of the swing, your body tenses up and you end up not hitting the ball or hitting it poorly. He called this over-concentration syndrome 'paralysis by analysis'. You can't be an effective golfer unless you can relax. An easy, well-coordinated swing is what gives you control over the ball.

Likewise, an easy, well-coordinated approach to your work is what enables you to be effective. If you find yourself terribly tense, stop and ask yourself what all that tension is accomplishing. Then slow down your pace. Move calmly and deliberately towards your goals. The relaxed, easy-does-it approach is a deceptively powerful one. Remember, activity is not productivity. When things do get hectic, one of the best tonics is to take a short break and just relax, physically and mentally. If you find yourself becoming overly tense while working, pause and try this exercise:

1. Assume a comfortable position. Loosen any tight clothing.

2. Close your eyes and imagine yourself sitting by a calm lake or stream with a picturesque mountain view. Feel the pleasant warmth of the sunlight on your face as you visualise this scene of total tranquillity. Empty your mind of all other thoughts.

3. Slowly let each part of your body go totally limp. Breathe deeply and concentrate on relaxing first your forehead and then your chin, neck, arms, torso and legs, in that order. Think of your body as a balloon with the air escaping from it and falling completely depleted.

4. Remain in this totally relaxed state for 10 minutes, or longer if you prefer. Remember that the keys to this exercise are total physical relaxation and emptying the mind of all thoughts and problems.

According to a group of Harvard University medical researchers, relaxation breaks on the job tend to improve a worker's overall health and job satisfaction by lowering blood pressure and frequency of headaches, and improving the ability to deal with others. This is one investment of time with a potentially high payoff.

Enjoy Your Work

You may be highly paid for what you do. Your job may come with generous holiday, medical and retirement benefits. However, if you don't enjoy what you are doing, can you consider yourself a success?

The most successful people I know are those who enjoy what they do while they are doing it. The real fun in life comes from total creative absorption in a task and not in the external rewards for doing it. When you enjoy your work, you feel a sense of harmony, purpose and comfort; and this sense of internal success will increase the odds of greater external rewards in the long run.

If you don't like your work, get out of it and find something you do enjoy. Obviously, all jobs have their pleasant and unpleasant aspects, but if you find the inherent nature of your work distasteful, you would be better off looking for greener pastures. Despite any present doubts you may have, I assure you you'll never regret it.

Recognise the Paradox of Perfection

The paradox of perfection is that by expecting perfection in yourself or others, you make a huge mistake. Most of us are immobilised by perfectionism more than we are aware of or are willing to admit. Our society has fed us large doses of the 'be perfect' injunction. Those who appear more perfect than others are held up as a model for all to see. 'See how smart Sarah is? She topped the class in commerce, and Paul did very well in his Mandarin exam. Aren't they terrific?'

There is nothing wrong with the pursuit of perfection at times. The problem is that too many of us apply perfectionism inappropriately. Perfection is necessary for some tasks, such as programming a computer, watchmaking or building ships in bottles. However, perfection isn't necessary for the vast majority of things we do in life. In these cases, perfectionism hinders effectiveness and wastes time and energy. Being compulsively perfectionist about your car, your house, your desk, your clothes, your children, your spouse, your colleagues and so on is a needless waste of time. It can keep you from achieving the important goals in your life.

The life of a perfectionist is not a happy one because they are trying to accomplish the impossible dream. More often than not, perfectionists are at odds with themselves because they can never live up to their own expectations.

Keep Your Perspective

A good rule of thumb to remember is that most things seem more important in the present than they actually are. The immediacy of the present tends to make us nearsighted. As you encounter pressure-inducing situations, keep the concept of the magnified present in mind. Is it really do or die? Is it really the chance of a lifetime? Back off and view things from a lifetime perspective. Most of the time you will find things far less drastic than they originally appeared. Such a realisation makes it easier to take things in your stride. Like everything else in life, effectiveness is largely a matter of attitude.

REMEMBER

Make sure you have the proper
tools for the job.

Work on improving your concentration
and memory skills.

Decision making is problem solving —
develop some strategies.

Prioritise and make every day count
by using your time effectively.

Overcome time-wasting habits
with effective scheduling.

Try to avoid overcommitting yourself
and learn to say no.

Work on developing some new attitudes
for effectiveness.

Keep control of effectiveness-killing
emotions such as guilt, worry,
fear, failure and anger.

PART 3

CONQUERING

TIME

WASTERS

CHAPTER 6

PUTTING AN END TO PUTTING IT OFF

If you want to make an easy job seem mighty hard, just keep putting off doing it.

OLIN MILLER

ARE YOU A procrastinator? If you answered yes, allow me to congratulate you for your honesty. To some degree, we all are. Procrastination is so universal, I hear there is now a Procrastination Club whose members have been planning to meet for some time but haven't gotten around to it yet.

THE PRICE OF PROCRASTINATION

Several of the work tapes discussed in Chapter 1 are underlying beliefs that can cause us to procrastinate. Myths such as activity means productivity, the easy way is the best way, work is inherently unpleasant, the justice myth and the myth that we work best under pressure give us plenty of reasons for delaying or not doing something.

Procrastination is often difficult to detect because it's a nonentity. The tasks you perform are what you get done, and the rest are left undone or are postponed. However, procrastination becomes a problem when you neglect or delay doing those things that are important to you.

We pay a gigantic price for the luxury of indulging ourselves in the lap of procrastination. It's the universal effectiveness-killer. Here are some ways in which 'putting it off' takes its enormous toll.

Waste of the Present

Dale Carnegie, author of such bestselling books as *How to Win Friends and Influence People*, wrote, 'One of the most tragic things I know about human nature is that all of us tend to put off living. We are all dreaming of some magical rose garden over the horizon — instead of enjoying the roses that are blooming outside our windows today.'

This is perhaps the greatest price of procrastination, because today is really all we have. All the talking, hoping and wishing about the future isn't making the most of the present and it certainly isn't building for the future. The past is history and tomorrow is only a vision, but the procrastinator wastes today. Worse yet, procrastination is terribly habit-forming and we can all guess what the procrastinator is going to do when tomorrow becomes today. The cycle will repeat itself and our procrastinator is on his (or her) way to . . .

An Unfulfilled Life

A fulfilled life means accomplishment and enjoyment each day. But procrastination is an immobiliser that blocks fulfilment. To the procrastinator there is always tomorrow, so today never has to count for anything. This creates a vacuum in the present, and many less desirable things appear to fill the void.

Boredom

If you know any boring people (and who doesn't?), you will usually find that they themselves are bored. You may choose to pity these people, but I don't. Boredom is a way of life and a great escape from using present moments constructively. If you want to be bored, that's your choice; but you'll never convince me that life is boring. Choosing boredom as a way of life is merely another way the procrastinator structures time.

The Anxiety of Working Under Pressure

By waiting until the last minute, procrastinators provide themselves with numerous opportunities to fill their life with anxieties. If you think such people are in short supply, go down to your local post office any afternoon at closing time and watch the traffic. If you didn't know better, you might think the government was giving away money rather than collecting it.

Impotent Goals

Many procrastinators, like doers, have goals. Of course, procrastinators never get around to pursuing their goals, much less achieving them. Consequently, their goals aren't really goals but rather just a lot of hot air. Such people are easily recognised by their chronic case of the 'I'm gonnas':

- ◆ I'm gonna go to Japan.
- ◆ I'm gonna get a better job.
- ◆ I'm gonna go back to university.
- ◆ I'm gonna buy a house.
- ◆ I'm gonna stop smoking.
- ◆ I'm gonna go on a diet.
- ◆ I'm gonna be my own boss someday.

The Constant Plague of Unsolved Problems

There are some problems in life that time and inaction can cure. However, the chronic procrastinator treats most, if not all, problems in this way. Ignoring or failing to recognise and deal with most problems doesn't make them go away. Rather, unsolved problems tend to create more problems. If you fail to fix a tiny leak in your roof, one day the whole ceiling will cave in. If you don't watch your weight, you will develop health complications. If you ignore the important but unpleasant aspects of your job, you may find yourself without one. Unsolved problems are much like cockroaches. If you don't make the effort to eradicate them, they can breed at an extremely high rate and compound your misery.

Continuous Frustration

Nobody likes being frustrated. Frustration is not getting what you want out of life. Who needs that? Evidently procrastinators must, because that's what they set themselves up for. Instead of taking action, they say to themselves, 'I hope', 'I wish' or 'Maybe things will get better'.

Let's consider as an example Anton, who should win a prize for continued frustration through inaction, if they ever have one. Anton has been working for a large company for over 20 years. He's about as dynamic as a dead fish. He doesn't like his 'dead-end job' as he calls it, his boss or the company. He doesn't like the city he lives in. But Anton isn't about to do anything drastic like change jobs or move to another city. He is hoping things will change of their own accord. Anton is a bachelor who has been going out with the same woman for over 10 years. She wants to get married. When the subject is brought up, Anton always replies, 'We're really just starting to get to know each other. Let's give it more time.'

Recently, Anton was evicted from his flat, where he had lived for several years. When asked why he had been evicted, Anton replied that he didn't like taking out the garbage; consequently, he didn't. One of his neighbours complained to the owner of a foul smell coming from Anton's flat, and she went to investigate. There she found count-less bags of garbage that Anton had accumulated. Both Anton and the garbage were put out in short order.

When last heard of, Anton was in a new flat and well on his way to building a new rubbish collection. However, we are not really concerned about Anton. He's going to get it all together — tomorrow, he hopes.

OTHER RESULTS OF PROCRASTINATION

Poor Health

Along with injury and premature death, this is another price we often pay for procrastinating. Sweeping the symptoms of medical problems under the rug and putting off getting them checked can be fatal.

Driving around for an extra week with bad tyres or worn-out brakes is another potential disaster area spawned by procrastinating. Important things are seldom urgent, until it's too late.

A Mediocre Career

This is still another price paid for the luxury of delay. Many procrastinators are content to stay in a lacklustre position or career that they really aren't suited for. Missed business opportunities often result from procrastination. If you delay calling on customers today, your competitor will take them away from you. If you delay updating your product, the competition will make you obsolete. Inaction leads to poor results or, even worse, to no results at all.

A Life of Indecision

Every decision is an opportunity to gain some control over your future. However, when you put off making decisions, you are forfeiting that opportunity. Sooner or later, circumstances will prevail and your right of choice will be taken away. By being indecisive you allow yourself to become a slave to your future rather than the master of it. This syndrome has ruined many managerial careers.

Poor Interpersonal Relationships

Poor relationships are another consequence of leading a life of inaction. Whenever a conflict arises, the procrastinator shies away from further contact rather than trying to resolve it amicably with the other person. If a conflict can't be resolved, the procrastinator still does nothing. Spending your career working for a boss you dislike, or staying in a bad marriage or sour relationship, is typical of the person of inaction. In addition to the frustration of clinging to bad relationships, the procrastinator simultaneously foregoes the opportunity to form happy and meaningful relationships.

Fatigue

This should come as no surprise. Although it may look easy, procrastination is not what it seems. It's an exhausting way to spend your time and energy. However, in the final analysis, it's the procrastinator's choice to be fatigued. They work hard all day struggling with doubt, indecision, delay, frustration and boredom. After all that, it's no wonder they are tired.

WHY WE PROCRASTINATE

Given that the price of procrastination is so high, it's only natural to ask, 'Why do we do it?' Most, but not all, reasons for procrastinating are emotional in nature.

To Escape an Overwhelming Task

By filling up present moments with trivia, we can escape doing something that we know is important but which seems too large to tackle. For example, Selina, a department manager, has to prepare a quarterly status report. She looks at the job and thinks: 'If I start this now, it's just going to be one interruption after another.' So she deludes herself into believing she'll do the report another day when she won't have to worry about interruptions, and spends the rest of her day writing meaningless memos, answering the telephone, chatting with colleagues and writing routine correspondence. She goes home tired but contented. After all, she got a lot done today! As the deadline date for the report approaches, Selina embarks on a crash program and ends up writing the report at night and over the weekend, complaining the whole time about how overworked she is. Even then, she's a week late in submitting it.

To Escape an Unpleasant Task

We all have important but unpleasant things to do from time to time. Given the choice between doing something pleasant and something unpleasant, we will usually choose the former.

Take the case of Charles. His garage is wall-to-wall chaos. On Saturday morning, Charles is given an ultimatum by his wife — clean out the garage this afternoon or sleep in it tonight. On his way out to the garage, Charles notices that his neighbour, Max, is having car trouble. Being a great lover of mechanics, and a good neighbour, Charles spends the next two hours helping Max fix his car. Then Max invites Charles in for a beer. It's the least he can do to thank Charles. Once inside, Max and Charles become absorbed in a rugby game on television.

After the game, Charles goes home and finds his wife in a foul temper. He ends up cleaning and organising the garage that night. The darkness hinders his efforts and he does a mediocre job, which gives him another payoff.

To Excuse Poor Work

This is one of the biggest cop-outs for delay. 'I just couldn't get to it until the last minute. If only I had had more time, I could have done a better job.' There is no more empty excuse than this one. There is never enough time in which to complete the available work. Time is limited. Work very seldom is, so our real choices must always be top priorities to which we allocate enough time to do the job effectively.

To Gain Sympathy

'See how hard I try?' is the battle cry of the procrastinating warrior. What it really means is: 'Don't see how little I have done.' Selina, looking haggard and overworked, turns in a half-baked report to her boss a week late. After stumbling around in the darkness for six hours, Charles drags himself indoors, covered from head to toe with dirt, and falls into bed, a picture of total fatigue. Anxiety-laden students beg their professor for an extension on their assignment deadline. And we are meant to feel sorry for these unfortunate victims of circumstance!

To Get Someone Else to do a Job

There's certainly nothing wrong with delegating most tasks. However, there are easier, quicker and more direct ways to go about it than playing the put-off game with someone. Such covert behaviour is a waste of everyone's time. Effective delegation is discussed in Chapter 9.

To Protect a Weak Self-image

A poor self-image and the accompanying fears of failure or success are other reasons for inaction. By deluding yourself with excuses for not doing something, you don't risk the anxiety and pain of failure. Simultaneously, you can avoid success and any problems that you fear may accompany it. You can just be your same old wonderful procrastinating self, complete with all the accompanying miseries, misfortunes and frustrations that you have had in the past. All of which adds up to one of the biggest emotional reasons for not doing something . . .

To Avoid Change

You spend your life being bored, critical, indecisive and lacking in achievement. And the best part is that you get to blame your misfortunes on everything and everyone but you. The easy-way tape plays on.

OTHER REASONS FOR PROCRASTINATION

Not all procrastination is bad, and not all of the reasons why we procrastinate are emotional cop-outs for inaction. There are several non-emotional reasons for procrastinating. I'll only mention them briefly here, because they have been discussed in detail previously:

◆

Improper goals can be one source of delay.
Are you sure this goal is still important to you
or necessary? Is it really your goal?

Insufficient information can prevent problems
from being solved, decisions from being made
and things from being done.

Goals without deadlines tend never to be achieved,
or are achieved much later than goals with deadlines.

Overcommitment inevitably leads to procrastination.
Saying yes to everything decreases the chances
of completing any one thing.

Unrealistic time estimates can cause bottlenecks
and delays. Remember Murphy's Law: everything
takes longer than you expect.

◆ — ◆ — ◆

TECHNIQUES FOR CREATING MOMENTUM

When Isaac Newton formulated his law of inertia, I'm sure he wasn't thinking about human behaviour. However, the law applies equally well to people and objects. A body (human or otherwise) at rest tends to remain at rest, and a body in motion tends to remain in motion.

When procrastinating you are at rest, and the hardest part is getting started. Once in motion, most of us will tend to remain in motion. I once heard the remark that the most difficult problem in life is getting out of a warm bed into a cold room. Once you get up, the day is underway. So it is with the other tasks in life. Gain momentum, and the task is well on its way to being completed.

The following list contains ideas for creating momentum. For any given task, one or more of them can help you to conquer procrastination.

◆ Recognise and acknowledge the futility of procrastination as a way of living. By procrastinating, you put yourself under a useless emotional strain. Do you really want a life of frustration, fatigue and boredom? Of course not. No one does. Admittedly, it's often hard to tackle difficult tasks, but what's your alternative? Spending your life rotting on the vine like an unpicked tomato may be your idea of living, but I seriously doubt it. You wouldn't be taking the time to read this book if you didn't value your life.

◆ Break down overwhelming tasks into small tasks. Anyone who has ever performed monumental feats knows the value of this idea. Henry Ford once remarked, 'Nothing is particularly hard if you divide it into small jobs.' It was on this idea that the auto assembly line was founded.

Do you want to write a 200-page book? Write a page a day and you will finish in less than seven months. Do you want to be a millionaire? Invest $1 000 a year starting at age 30 and get a 15 per cent compounded annual return. At age 65, you will have a million dollars.

Whenever you are confronted with a seemingly overwhelming task, divide it into as many five- or 10-minute subtasks as you can think of. Write them down and list them in the order to be performed. Tackle the first one now. When you can spare another five or 10 minutes, do another, and so on. Once you get started, you'll gain the momentum to finish the job. Large successes are usually a series of small ones. 'A journey of a thousand miles begins with one step.'

◆ Face unpleasant tasks squarely. A humourist once defined an optimist as someone who leaves the dinner dishes because they will feel more like washing them in the morning. Most unpleasant tasks are like the dinner dishes. Ignoring them doesn't make them disappear and usually makes things worse. Why keep clouding your horizons when a little effort will get you sunny skies? One way to tackle an unpleasant task is to reserve a small amount of time, say 10 or 15 minutes, and resolve to work on it at that time and quit when your time is up. Large problems such as preparing a budget, taking an inventory or cleaning out the garage can be handled in this way.

Unfortunately, some unpleasant tasks don't lend themselves to this approach. Tasks such as firing an employee or being the bearer of bad news can't usually be handled in a piecemeal manner. In such cases, your best choice is to do it and get it over with. Not doing it today only ensures that you will feel equally burdened with it and other tasks tomorrow. Realise that you are merely compounding your workload with inaction and then resolve to do the task — now.

◆ Do a start-up task. Sometimes a little spontaneous physical action is all you need to get you in the mood to start a major task. Do you have a yard full of leaves to rake? Walk down to the corner shop and buy some lawn leaf bags — now. Do you have a report to write? Take a piece of paper and make a list of 10 major points you wish to include and rank them in the order in which you plan to discuss them — now. Have you been putting off answering a letter? Address the envelope — now. Do you need to settle a misunderstanding with a customer? Look up his telephone number — now.

◆ Take advantage of your moods. How many times have you said to yourself, 'I'm just not in the mood'? The idea here is to use your moods to your advantage. For example, you may not feel like writing that report today, but do you feel like calling someone who can give you some helpful information? You may not feel like repairing the broken TV antenna, but do you feel like gathering the necessary hardware? Remember those things you have been delaying and put your moods to work for you rather than against you.

◆ Think of something important that you have been putting off. List the good things that could possibly happen by doing the task. Now list all the disadvantages that could come about as a result of inaction. You will usually find that the advantages of action far outweigh the liabilities of inaction. Such a technique helps to create the enthusiasm to get you going.

For example, let's suppose it's spring. You want to plant a vegetable garden in your backyard, but just can't seem to get around to it. Your list might look something like the following:

ADVANTAGES OF ACTION	DISADVANTAGES OF INACTION
1. Fresh-tasting, home-grown vegetables are a real treat.	1. Time is running out. If I don't start soon, I won't get another chance.
2. With the additional saving in grocery money, we can afford a trip to Bali.	2. Without the garden, we will have to content ourselves with a cheaper holiday.
3. Growing a garden is good exercise and a great diversion from my job.	3. Without some additional diversions, I'll probably spend my spare time worrying about my job.
4. This is an opportunity to learn by doing something I've never done before.	4. I'm getting a little old to believe in the Jolly Green Giant. Lonely is a man without his own niblets.
5. I can make this a family project that we can all learn from, enjoy, participate and take pride in. This can bring us all closer.	5. We all seem to be drifting in separate directions. Without some common goals, family unity can be severely damaged.

◆ Make a commitment to someone or a wager with someone. Tell your boss that you will have the budget prepared a week early or you will buy him lunch at a restaurant of his choice. If you are a sales representative, bet your colleagues that you will increase your last month's sales by 20 per cent or buy all the drinks at a future happy hour. If you bet with someone, be sure there's something in it for you if you win. You want both an incentive for reaching your goal and a penalty for falling short.

◆ Give yourself a reward. This is one of my favourite methods for conquering procrastination because it's positive in nature. Find an important goal that you have been dodging and decide what would be a fitting reward for you when you achieve it. For example, you might decide to get that new briefcase you've been admiring after you add 10 customers to your list. Or how about a new pair of shoes after cleaning out the garage or shampooing the rugs? Make your reward system commensurate with the size of the task. For example, if you have been studying a correspondence course at night to secure an advanced degree, promise yourself something really nice, like two weeks in the Whitsundays after graduation.

Besides being a lot of fun, setting up your own reward system can be a very effective way of cutting down on procrastination. Just be honest with yourself. If you do the task, be sure to give yourself the reward; and if you don't complete the task, don't reward yourself.

◆ For rational delays, the following methods will help:

— Give yourself deadlines.

— Get more information.

— Avoid overcommitment.

— Set realistic time schedules.

◆ Resolve to make every day count. Your life is too short to waste on inaction. Before you get up in the morning, resolve to do two things: enjoy today, and do something that will make for a better tomorrow. Every day is a treasure. Treat it as such and you will take a big step towards ending procrastination.

◆ Be decisive and have the courage to act. A good working definition of courage is the ability to act when you are afraid.

Take the case of David. David was a 50-year-old chief engineer with a wife and family. For 10 years, he had been planning to open his own manufacturing concern. He had a product, a good market, technical expertise, capital and potential cust-omers lined up. However, he just wouldn't make that final commitment to open his own business. David was overwhelmed by a case of the 'what ifs': 'What if the whole thing goes belly up?' 'What if I can't send the kids to a private school?' 'What if I can't pay the mortgage?' and so on. He was being held back by fear.

With the encouragement of his wife and children, David made the big move and opened his own business, where he has been successful both personally and financially. His only regrets are the years of enjoyment and satisfaction he missed by not going into business earlier.

By delaying action, you waste valuable time and, as David found out, all the money in the world cannot buy back one moment (much less years) of lost time. It's gone forever.

Remember, you're better than you think and can take much more adversity than you ever dreamed of. Cure yourself of such self-defeating statements as 'I'm gonna,' 'I wish,' 'I want' and 'I hope'. Make something happen! Your actions will speak for themselves.

◆ Refuse to be bored. Are you living in a rut? Get out of it. Drive another way to work. Eat lunch at a different restaurant. Change your hairstyle or buy some new clothes. Find an exotic food you're afraid of and purposely order or cook some. Replace the familiar with the unfamiliar. As Auntie Mame said, 'Life is a banquet.' So why sit in a corner each day with a can of sardines? There's so much to experience and so little time.

◆ Practise doing absolutely nothing. When you find you are avoiding an important task, sit still in a chair and see how long you can go without doing anything. You will probably find yourself eager to get moving in a matter of minutes. Most of us are rather poor at the art of doing nothing. When you can no longer stand the interlude of nothingness, resolve to tackle that job you've been avoiding, and begin it — now.

◆ Frequently ask yourself, 'What's the best use of my time and energy right now?' If the answer is not what you are doing at the moment, stop that and put your time and energy to work on a more important task.

◆ Finally, ask yourself these two questions each morning:

— What is my greatest opportunity today and how can I make the most of it?

— What is the greatest problem facing me today and what can I do to overcome it?

CHAPTER 7

MINIMISING INTERRUPTIONS

A committee is a group of men who individually can do nothing but collectively can meet and decide that nothing can be done.
ALFRED E. SMITH

'OF COURSE, I'LL serve on the committee. You can always count on me.' 'My door is always open.' 'I'm as close as your telephone whenever you need me.' What these statements have in common is that they each can be translated into a fourth: 'I'd love to waste my time. When do we start?'

What's that? You disagree? You say you are paid to do these things? If you are being rewarded for being available rather than being effective, then your organisation's priorities are not results-oriented. Unfortunately, the growth of massive bureaucracies is providing more jobs with a lesser premium on results. Activities, rituals, pastimes and meaningless red tape have become the yardsticks for performance.

Nevertheless, productive people want to produce, and it offends the very essence of their being to do otherwise. Are you someone who abhors committee meetings and has an equally strong distaste for being continuously on tap for random telephone calls and drop-in visitors? If so, God bless you. You have a basic predisposition towards effectiveness. Given half an opportunity you will likely work less, accomplish more and do something meaningful with your life.

Meetings, visitors and telephone calls are not necessarily unproductive, any more than gunpowder is a necessarily destructive substance. It's all a matter of application. Unfortunately, the seeming legitimacy of these common time-wasters allows them to proliferate unchecked. If we take steps to make judicious use of meetings, visitors and the telephone, these time-wasters can become tools to aid effectiveness. Let's consider them one at a time.

WHY WE HAVE SO MANY USELESS MEETINGS

When it comes to meetings, most of us behave as though we had never heard that time is money. Meetings are terribly expensive, and most of us believe that this is the number one time-waster. How much does a meeting cost? Calculate the per-hour salaries of those on a committee and add them up. It's very common to have meetings that cost thousands of dollars an hour. However, most of us don't tend to think of meetings in terms of dollars and cents. Consequently, one reason for so many useless meetings is that we fail to recognise the cost. Other popular reasons for holding meetings follow.

To Provide an Audience for Someone

Some people like to hear themselves talk so much that they just have to share it with a group. How many meetings have you been to where all you did was listen to someone's views on everything from world economics to the mating of Great Danes with Chihuahuas? Far too many, I'm sure. It's a very ex-pensive ego trip, but it's one reason that we have so many useless meetings.

To Socialise

There are very few of us who can tolerate working alone for extended periods of time. Meetings provide a great excuse for us to get together and quell any pangs of loneliness we feel. In addition to conducting business, Ray can talk to Bill about his golf game and Anna can check which of her colleagues want to join in a skiing weekend. Everyone would be better off if they just threw a party, but that's only for special occasions.

We can't afford to admit to ourselves that we aren't getting anything done, so we meet and socialise under the guise of committee work.

To Escape from Being Effective

Meetings are an excuse for poor work or no work at all. You can volunteer for many committees and fill up virtually all your time serving on them. This gives you a perfect excuse for ignoring the most important aspects of your job. Better yet, you can dodge unpleasant tasks or turn in assignments late and say you were too busy to get around to them last week because your time was taken up in meetings. Since meetings are an acceptable way to structure work time, you appear to be an ambitious, caring soul with many irons in the fire. The fact that your time would have been better spent holidaying in Tasmania is of no consequence. The activity myth strikes again.

Habit

The only real reason for having many meetings is that it's always been that way. Regularly scheduled meetings are often prime candidates for wasting time.

People are usually resistant to change. As a result, traditions tend to live on long after their purpose has passed. In government there are hundreds of special committees, working on all manner of things. Every government at some time says it is going to do something about them, but they still exist. They exist not because of a real need but because of tradition. Their existence pacifies some section of the community or government.

To Pass the Buck

Very often a decision can and should be made by a particular individual, but they are reluctant to do so. Instead, they form committees and automatically adopt their recommendations. If the decision meets with an ill fate, the buck can be passed to the committee and no one person is held responsible. Such a strategy is frequently utilised by members of the CYA (or 'Cover Your Arse Club'). 'Something that is everyone's responsibility is no one's responsibility . . . Is it any wonder that many institutions are so ineptly managed? The places are largely run by committees.'

Of course, people who delegate decisions to a committee aren't actually avoiding responsibility. They are still accountable for the decisions, so they only fool themselves if they delegate, thinking they have passed the buck.

To Fool People into Believing They are Participating in Important Decisions

Many committees do make use of the capabilities of people to make important decisions. However, all too often the boss forms a committee to make recommendations and then does whatever he (or she) wants or, worse yet, tells the committee what kind of recommendation to make. The meetings are usually held in the spirit of 'All in favour say "aye", all opposed say "fired".' Such pseudo-participation is only a waste of everyone's time. Why ask for advice if your mind is made up?

GETTING THE MOST FROM MEETINGS

Hendrik van Loon, the American historian, once defined a committee as 'a group which succeeds in getting something done only when it consists of three members, one of whom happens to be sick and another absent'. Fortunately, it doesn't have to be that way. With a little forethought and diligence, we can eliminate many useless meetings and make the remaining ones more effective. The following ideas are presented with those purposes in mind.

General Guidelines

◆ Begin by taking an inventory of all existing committees and meetings held. Write down the purpose of each. Are they really necessary? Have some outlived their usefulness? Can any be consolidated or eliminated? If so, do it.

◆ Have a minimum number of standing committees. No committee should be allowed to linger on indefinitely. Regularly question the purpose of each committee's existence.

◆ Every time you form a committee, state its purpose, give it a deadline for achieving its purpose, if possible, and dissolve it when it has achieved its goal.

◆ Never go to a meeting if you can send someone else.

◆ Keep the number of members attending as small as possible.

Large committees get very cumbersome and usually end up being dominated by a small number of people.

◆ Never call a meeting when there is a reasonable alternative. Can a conference call be arranged instead? Can the job be done by someone else?

Preparation

Working smart in meetings is much like the rest of life. An investment of time and energy in forethought and planning pays handsome dividends.

◆ If you decide to call a meeting, pin down precisely what you expect to accomplish at the meeting. Meetings should have at least one goal and, if there is more than one goal, a set of priorities.

◆ Set a starting and ending time for meetings and resolve to stick to them. If people arrive late, begin without them. With respect to scheduling, it's a good idea to schedule meetings back to back, before lunch or near the end of the day. This often prevents long, drawn-out meetings.

◆ Prepare an agenda and circulate it well in advance to those who will be attending. On the agenda list the goals, topics to be covered, and time of beginning and ending. It also helps to provide participants with background reading material prior to the meeting so that they can be prepared to discuss the issue without wasting meeting time.

◆ Prepare exhibits that help to clarify or illustrate the points you wish to make. Charts, graphs, handouts, overhead transparencies and whiteboards can all be helpful. Provide notepads and pens for the participants. Check out the physical surroundings for comfort, size, lighting and ventilation.

Execution

Many meetings only result in another one being called. The following guidelines can help to make meetings more effective for all concerned.

◆ Prepare and stick to the agenda. Stay on course. Focus on the purpose of the meeting and the topic that has the floor. Meetings can easily get sidetracked or degenerate into general discussions. It's the responsibility of the chairperson to prevent this from happening.

Another related problem is that some people like to complicate issues and problems during meetings. I have seen a motion get amended so many times that the participants don't know what they're voting on. Try to handle issues singly, and discourage ambiguous and trivial complications.

◆ If you are invited to attend a meeting and feel you have nothing to contribute, don't go. If you can't get out of it, bring something else to do at the meeting. Meetings can command the presence of your body but they will only waste your time if you allow them to.

Catch up on your reading or write letters if it's a large meeting. If the meeting is one at which you have to look as if you're paying attention, you can play the role by looking intelligent while thinking about other important matters. No one will ever know the difference. When someone you greatly admire and respect appears to be thinking deep thoughts, they are probably thinking about lunch.

◆ If you are conducting a meeting, excuse those who have finished making their contribution before the meeting is over. If you are attending and have made your contribution, ask to be excused.

◆ If you are chairing a meeting, it's your responsibility to try and involve everyone in the discussion. If some people are reluctant to speak, ask them for an opinion. Usually, however, the problem is someone who talks too much and often gets sidetracked. If this is the case, calmly keep discussing the issue at hand and stick to your agenda.

If you find that people are bored or bogged down with the issue at hand, tactical sidetracking can sometimes get things going. The idea here is to get off the track completely, but the purpose is to get people to open up. Once they seem to be more receptive and enthusiastic, go back to the agenda.

◆ Sometimes meetings drag on because people are just too comfortable to get up. If so, consider holding a stand-up meeting. It's amazing how quickly things can get done when people aren't sitting around being comfortable. As a more subtle alternative, you might consider using less comfortable chairs. This is an old trick employed by some restaurants to prevent customers from tying up tables for hours.

Follow-up

Don't neglect to follow up on decisions made at meetings. Here are some suggestions for following up.

◆ Have someone present to take accurate and relevant minutes at the meetings. It's best if this isn't one of the participants but rather a third party such as an assistant. The minutes should be recorded, duplicated and sent to all participants as soon as possible. After a few days, most of us remember only a small fraction of what transpired at a meeting. A good recording system is essential.

◆ Prepare a checklist before each meeting stating what you want to accomplish. At the end of the meeting, compare the results with the original agenda. This can serve as a benchmark for measuring the effectiveness of meetings.

In summary, the effectiveness of meetings is best enhanced by eliminating or avoiding the useless ones. Practically every organisation has its share of meetings, some of which should be avoided like the plague. Assuming certain meetings are necessary, they should focus on goals, and their contribution to the achievement of goals should be assessed.

DEALING WITH DROP-IN VISITORS

One of the main problems of the work world is drop-in visitors. It's quite common for many of us to spend half or more of our workday dealing with unexpected visitors. Others of us make our living by playing the role of a visitor. If you are a sales representative, such is the nature of your job.

Like meetings, drop-in visitors give us all sorts of excuses to be ineffective. We can socialise, provide an audience, ask others for their ideas (when our mind is usually made up anyway) and practise the art of procrastination with all of its wonderful payoffs.

Of course, visitors are often necessary. Many of them keep us informed and provide us with ideas that enable us to be more effective. My recommendation is that you minimise the unnecessary ones and schedule necessary visits so that they don't cause random havoc to your workday. With that basic policy in mind, here are some ways to manage drop-in visits:

◆ Pin down who your main drop-ins are. Keep a visitor log for a week or two, and write down the names of your visitors and how much of your time they take up. Usually you will find the 80/20 rule holds true: 80 per cent of your time spent in visits will be taken up by 20 per cent, or less, of your drop-in visitors. Once you know who your main interrupters are, you will be better able to devise a strategy for accommodating and/or minimising their visits.

◆ Close your door. This might be a problem if you are in a supervisory or managerial position. Leadership and supervisory training programs stress the importance of managers being available to confer with subordinates. However, an open-door policy was never to be construed as managers always having to drop whatever they are doing to entertain visitors. Being accessible is important, but always being accessible is a blueprint for wasting time.

An open door invites people roaming the corridors to come in and waste your time. If you can't understand why you have to work such long hours, try closing your door for a good part of your day. It works wonders.

◆ Remove any extra chairs and other social amenities from your office. If your office contains a number of chairs or if it's equipped with a coffee pot, you may be playing the role of informal host in your job. People will think of your office as a gathering spot for a chat. While it's important to be sociable, you are probably being paid to do a good deal more than that. If you are playing host and are still on top of things, there's no cause for alarm. However, if you love to socialise and you find yourself falling behind, inform your friends of the problem and remove that coffee pot from your office. If they are really your friends, they will understand.

◆ If someone wants to talk with you, volunteer to go to their office to chat. Such a practice gives you control over the length of the visit. As soon as business is transacted, you can get up and go back to your office. Drop-in visitors can't tie up your time if they don't get the chance to drop in.

◆ If someone walks into your office unexpectedly, stand up and remain standing. Such body language usually indicates to the other party that you're busy and have more pressing things to do. Allowing drop-ins to sit down only increases the likelihood of their staying too long.

◆ Rearrange your desk and chair so that you aren't facing the door. If your door is open but your back is to it, the office socialites will be less likely to drop in.

◆ If someone knocks on your door, confer with them outside your office. Once again, the idea is to keep visitors from firmly planting themselves in your office.

◆ Position your assistant's desk where they can screen your unexpected visitors. A good assistant can handle many routine questions and problems and greatly reduce your time spent with drop-in visitors.

◆ Schedule visiting hours and see visitors only at those times, unless there is an emergency. Your assistant can schedule appointments for visitors and inform you about the nature and purpose of their visit.

◆ Be candid with visitors. If someone drops in and asks if you're busy, answer 'Yes'. If you can see them for only five minutes, tell them so. If they need to see you for further discussion, arrange an appointment.

◆ Once a visitor is in your office, you can control the length of the visit in several ways. If you feel a visitor has transacted their business and is overstaying, simply be quiet. Don't contribute to a needless conversation and there won't be one. Another way is to ask your assistant, prior to the visit, to interrupt you, buzz you, or walk in and remind you of a meeting or another appointment (real or imagined). Of course, you can simply say that you have to be at a meeting in 10 minutes and bring the visit to a close.

◆ Build time into your schedule to allow for unexpected visitors. No matter how much you plan, scheme and screen visitors, some will inevitably get through. Keeping a loose schedule, as was previously mentioned, is the best way to prevent the unexpected from hindering your effectiveness.

◆ Use your coffee breaks or lunch hours to meet with visitors. Many visitors have important and necessary reasons for conferring with you. Meeting these people for mid-morning breaks or luncheons makes multiple use of time. Many high-level executives schedule regular luncheons with their assistants or colleagues for the purpose of exchanging information. It's an idea all of us can use if we are plagued with an overabundance of visitors.

MAKING THE TELEPHONE WORK FOR YOU

Do you suffer from telephonitis? Most of us do. It's a disease of epidemic proportions that can waste much time, energy and money. More often than not, the disease isn't contagious and is caused by curiosity and a lack of self-discipline on the part of the victim.

It's always great fun to be interrupted from the task at hand by the ringing or buzzing of the telephone. Who could it be? What do they want? The mystery of the unknown is always more appealing than attending to the task at hand. So we take the calls as they come and allow our work to be randomly disrupted.

Actually, telephonitis is the result of a good thing put to misuse. The following ideas can help you to prevent or cure this dreadful effectiveness-killer.

◆ Log your calls for one week. Write down who called, when they called, what they wanted and the length of time spent on the telephone. Log your outgoing calls in a similar manner. The 80/20 rule will probably apply — 80 per cent of your calls come from less than 20 per cent of all callers. After you have completed a week's log, answer the following questions:

— Who called?

— Who did you call?

— Which calls were important?

— How many calls could have been handled by someone else?

— How much time was spent on unnecessary calls?

◆ Make your telephone a time- and energy-saver. That's why it's there. The telephone is a terrific labour-saving tool. Proper use of it is one of our greatest effectiveness tools. You can use it for conference calls, rather than attending time-consuming meetings. You can use the telephone instead of writing letters. The cost of clerical help is increasing, while the cost of telephone calls is decreasing. The telephone gets you information in minutes that a letter could take weeks to acquire. You can also use the telephone to save the time and expense of trips.

◆ Establish a period of time each day for placing and receiving telephone calls. For most of us, the best time is in the morning, when people are most likely to be in their offices. Encourage your regular callers to call during those hours.

◆ Have your assistant screen your calls. This can be done tactfully without making you seem inaccessible. Your assistant can say to the party, 'She's rather tied up at the moment. Would you like me to interrupt her or may I have her call you back?' Your assistant can also provide information to callers on routine matters, thus eliminating your need to call back.

◆ Outline the information you want or wish to impart before placing outgoing calls. This will clarify the main points in your mind and you will be less likely to forget to discuss one of your reasons for calling.

◆ Buy a small, three-minute hourglass and put it by your phone. Every time you get a call or make one, see if you can successfully complete it in three minutes. Don't rush, but keep a score card and see if you can reduce your telephone time each week. Make a game out of it and reward yourself each week that you reduce your telephone time.

◆ When you place a call, set the tone of the conversation at the outset. Ask to speak to the party and tell them who is calling. Once you get your party on the line, minimise the small talk and get right to, 'The reason I'm calling you . . .'

◆ If you take the time to place or take a call, give the other person your undivided attention. Don't shuffle papers, or speak to others around you or allow yourself to be distracted. You can do only one thing well at a time. If you are interrupted, ask the other party if they would like to hold or if you can call them back. To keep others waiting unnecessarily is inconsiderate. They are busy too, and your lack of consideration could alienate them.

◆ Once you have transacted business, bring the conversation to a polite and prompt close. If you get a long-winded caller, tell them you have a pressing appointment. If that doesn't work, hang up while you are talking. It's not polite to hang up while *they* are talking, but it's socially acceptable to do so while *you* are. If they have anything important to say, they will call back. If not, they will probably go and bother someone else.

◆ Get a telephone answering machine. This is a terrific screening device for the home or office. In addition to screening calls, they answer your telephone when you can't, or are busy and don't want to be interrupted, so you need never miss a call. Most models also have an optional attachment that plays back your messages to you if you call your machine while you're away from the home or office. If you don't like answering machines, use an answering service.

One final thought about interruptions. You can't be interrupted if you can't be found. Therefore . . .

GET YOURSELF A HIDEAWAY

When you have important tasks to do and find yourself in dire need of solitude, it's comforting to know that there is somewhere you can readily have it. Tell only those who need to know where you are going, and proceed to hibernate.

Hideaways can come in various shapes and sizes, depending on your purpose and the amount of time you need there. The following are some possible avenues you can consider when the need arises for a temporary escape from all interruptions.

- ◆ Your company may have rooms set aside to provide solitude for people who need to work undisturbed.
- ◆ Libraries are readily available places where you can work undisturbed.
- ◆ Arrange to swap offices with someone who works for another company. Such an arrangement can be beneficial to both parties if you both have a frequent need for solitude.
- ◆ You can escape to a hotel or motel — the further away the better. Try to go where no one knows you.
- ◆ Renting an apartment is an excellent idea if you need a great deal of uninterrupted solitude. I know a professor who does this. As a result, he has written several bestselling textbooks and made himself a small fortune. He rents an efficiency apartment where the other tenants in the complex spend their days at work. The professor works on his books in the morning when the complex is like a tomb. His afternoons are spent teaching and seeing students, and he leaves the evenings free to enjoy his family.
- ◆ You can always use your car as a temporary hideaway. Drive to a secluded spot and do your working or thinking in your car. This option is often overlooked.

The point is that there are many avenues for escaping interruptions and keeping them from disrupting your life. With a little thought and imagination, you can discover those that will work for you.

CHAPTER 8

WINNING THE PAPER WAR

Xerox: A trademark for
a photocopying device
that can make rapid reproductions
of human error, perfectly.
MERLE L. MEACHAM

DURING HIS CAREER with NASA, in the United States, Wernher von Braun remarked, 'We can lick gravity, but sometimes the paperwork is overwhelming.' Stop and think about how paper has woven itself into the very fabric of our lives. We wake up to the morning paper and, for most of us, paper is to our occupations what bread is to our diets — a fattening staple.

Just as time is money, paper is money. Let's suppose you own a small business whose rate of profit on sales is 10 per cent. Your paper workload has increased and you have to hire another clerk at a salary of $400 a week, or $20 000 a year. To pay the salary of that clerk, you now have to increase your yearly sales revenue by $200 000. And that's not including fringe benefits. Are you starting to get the picture? On the other hand, $20 000 saved is $20 000 earned and is a direct addition to profit.

Worse than the monetary costs are the needless waste of time and energy created by the overuse of paper. It takes time to fill out forms, write memos, read computer printouts, prepare budgets, write reports, make 14 photocopies, and read faxes and the mail.

CAUSES OF THE PAPER WAR

Rare, indeed, is the employed person who doesn't feel somewhat affected by the paper war. We all agree that we have to deal with too much paperwork. If no one seems to like all this paperwork, it's only logical to ask why there is so much of it.

The General Information Explosion

Industry in our society is surely dominated by the information industry. Broadly defined, the information industry covers all of those businesses that do not make products. More than 60 per cent of our entire working population works in the information industry, and this percentage is increasing rapidly. Our knowledge has been increasing at an incredible rate. An engineer or scientist who doesn't keep up with the state of the art is obsolete in less than five years. Much the same holds true for many other technical and non-technical fields. Each year, thousands of new book titles are published. Add to this the countless number of newspapers, journals and pamphlets published, and you have a major contributor to the paper war.

Photocopiers

Photocopiers are another major factor. Practically every office has some type of photocopy machine. If you're going to run off five copies, why not run off seven or eight? Who knows — you may need them. It's this type of thinking that causes our effectiveness to drown in our own clutter.

Insecurity

Once again, it's our old work myth: if you create a lot of paper work for yourself and others, then everyone gets to keep busy and no one has to feel guilty about not having enough work to do. Busy hands are happy hands. An idle mind is the devil's workshop. Just keep shuffling those papers.

We Don't Trust Each Other

Everyone wants everything in writing. The popular notion in today's society is 'Don't trust anybody'. Perhaps with good cause we have adopted mistrust as a common societal value. However, the fact is that if more than a small percentage of us were totally untrustworthy, the very foundations of our society would shake. We may not realise it but we are all highly dependent on each other.

Somehow we feel much safer if things are in writing. This feeling has been so magnified that we spend much of our time documenting and verifying details of little or no consequence, and seeing to it that everyone gets a copy.

The Proliferation of Computers

Along with EDP (electronic data pollution), the growing use of computers has contributed to the proliferation of paper. This is despite claims that computers would lead to paperless offices. Some computers print out at the rate of thousands of lines a minute, making it very easy for users to generate reams of data reports as well as numerous pieces of junk mail and other documents.

HOW TO WIN THE WAR

The chances of any one person winning any but their own paper war are much like the chances of melting an iceberg with a match. The proliferation of computers and photocopiers, and the quest for knowledge mean that you can almost certainly count on having to contend with even more paper in the future. However, this doesn't prevent you from taking a number of positive steps to protect yourself from the storm. The following ideas will require awareness, recognition and change with respect to how you deal with paper. Paper use, like time use, is mainly habit and many habits are effectiveness-killers. Winning the paper war, like charity, starts at home and begins with getting your own house in order.

If You Don't Like the Paper War, Don't Contribute to It

You wouldn't declare war on your worst enemy and then provide them with ammunition. Take a similar approach with unnecessary paper.

Declare war on it and make your first strategy to generate as little paper as possible.

◆ Begin by focusing on the results you hope to achieve. Your purpose is to get results, not to shuffle paper. If picking up a piece of paper and acting on it furthers your achievement, go ahead and take care of it. If not, put it aside or, better yet, throw it away. Such an approach will find you eliminating a good amount of unnecessary paper.

◆ Put only the bare necessities in writing. Why send out memos when face-to-face communication will get your meaning across better? Whenever you are tempted to document something, ask yourself, 'What's the worst that can happen by not recording this?' If the answer isn't too bad, don't record it. All too often, information that we document is being documented in other places as well. A great deal of unnecessary paper is the result of needless duplication. If someone writes you a letter requesting information, answer it on their letter. This will cut your clerical expense as well as correspondence time.

◆ Screen yourself from unnecessary paper. Prepare a priority list of paper work that you should handle and have your assistant handle the routine paper chores, sort out paper that needs your attention and rank items in order of importance. Ask to have your name removed from any unnecessary reading, mailing and subscription lists.

◆ Don't be a 'copycat'. Photocopiers hinder our effectiveness, although they are designed to do the opposite. Every time you are tempted to make an extra copy, remember the excess baggage that you are creating for yourself and others.

◆ 'If in doubt, throw it out' was the motto of Marks & Spencer, a large British retail chain who declared war on paper. Deciding that paper work was becoming cost-prohibitive, they launched a campaign to simplify, eliminate and throw away unnecessary paper. Store managers were given more autonomy and fewer procedures to adhere to. Company financial reporting was less concerned with perfectionist to-the-penny accounting and more with reasonable approximations. Within two years, Marks & Spencer did away with 22 million forms weighing 105 tons. Morale, profits and productivity all increased.

Never underestimate the value of a wastepaper basket. It's rapidly becoming more and more necessary for success in any endeavour.

Go through your files twice a year and throw out the unessential, outdated items. Don't file or keep any piece of paper unless you think it's absolutely necessary.

◆ 'Try to handle each piece of paper only once' is one of Alan Lakein's best rules for winning the paper war. If you pick up a piece of paper, don't put it down without doing something that will help move it on its way. If you can throw it away, that's the best alternative. If it needs a reply, answer it. The main idea is to do something, no matter how small, to get the paper behind you. Every time you pick up a piece of paper needing your action, failing to act only means you'll have to double the time and energy you spend on it by picking it up again.

If you find yourself shuffling the same piece of paper, mark it with a dot every time you pick it up. As the dots start to accumulate, you will be reminded to move the paper on its way before it looks like it has the measles.

◆ Use the telephone. Many of us grew up in another era when the cost of communicating via long-distance telephone calls was prohibitive. Today things are quite different. A long-distance call, in addition to eliminating paper, saves time by getting an instant response. In addition, you can ask questions or paraphrase the other party to ensure that you understand each other.

◆ Master the art of dictating. Many effective people keep on top of their written correspondence by using a dictation recorder. Letters can be transcribed about five times faster than they can be written out in long-hand. Additionally, this can be done while waiting for appointments or travelling to and from work. Previously unproductive minutes can become almost effortlessly productive.

If you have trouble dictating your thoughts, keep your sentences and paragraphs short. Another method is to record a description of what you want to say and have your assistant compose a letter from your description.

If your work entails a great deal of correspondence, I highly recommend a dictating machine, even if it means purchasing it at your own expense. It's an investment in your future aimed at increasing your effectiveness. If you aren't willing to invest in yourself, why should anyone else? In the final analysis, everyone is in business for themselves.

◆ Start a war on paper in your office. Talk about it with your boss, your subordinates and your colleagues. They are probably as fed up with the paper war as you are. Create a list of ways to cut down on the use of paper. Have a 'throwing out' contest. Give the person who throws out the most paper a free lunch. Provide an incentive for not using the photocopier to excess. Recognise and reward someone who comes up with a new idea for significantly saving paper. Remember, paper is money. Lee Grossman, a management consultant whose speciality is paper-work problems, believes that costs could be cut by 20 per cent if paper shuffling were brought under control. Cutting any company's costs by 20 per cent would really light up the financial scoreboard.

These are some of the things you can do to cut down on your active participation in the paper war. Many paper-work tasks are completely unnecessary, and how effectively we handle them brings us back to the basics of writing and reading. A few words about each are in order.

HOW TO WRITE LESS
AND COMMUNICATE MORE

Many people passionately hate to write anything, be it a memo, letter or report. One reason for this is that they are poor writers. It doesn't have to be that way, and the problem can usually be corrected with a little patience and practice.

'So what makes a poor writer?' you ask. A poor writer is someone who cannot or will not make themselves easily understood. There are several main reasons why poor writing abounds.

First, we inherited many poor writing practices from our ancestors. Flowery, verbose, bombastic language was considered a sign of literacy and culture in the 19th century. To say 'He propelled the prolate spheroid' was judged superior to saying 'He threw the ball.' Much of our training in schools at all levels encourages us to use long words and flowery phrases when simplicity would communicate better. There is still a lot of leftover 19th century baggage hanging around the ivory towers. The 20th century is a very different era, characterised by rapid change and great scientific and technical complexity. Things are tough enough to understand without hiding them in a cloud of syllables.

Another reason we have poor writing is the need to impress each other with our vocabularies. The writers of academic papers and articles are often guilty of making simple, obvious concepts appear difficult.

Disorganised thinking is another cause of poor writing. In as much as writing is an expression of thought, confused thinking leads to confused writing. Related to this is the attempt to hide ignorance or poor solutions to problems in an entanglement of verbiage. Smoke-screening your thoughts will fool only the most gullible of readers. The others may not understand you, but most of them will realise that you don't want them to.

Improving your writing is much like learning to swim or play golf, in that you learn by doing. Writing to communicate also involves intelligence, common sense and abandoning any childhood tapes you may be clinging to telling you what a poor writer you are. The ground rules are simple and straightforward. Here they are:

◆ Get organised. What are you writing? A letter? A report? A memo? Who is it for? What is the central point you are trying to communicate? What other points do you wish to make? Do they relate to the main point? If so, how?

   If you have to write a lengthy report, plan and write an outline first. This will be time well spent. Gathering and organising your facts before you begin to write makes for much smoother writing.

◆ Use plenty of paper if you prefer to do a handwritten or typed draft than compose at the computer. Double- or triple-space the lines. This way you can make revisions on your first draft without having to rewrite the entire thing (unless you deem it necessary). In the long run, you save time, energy and paper. Giving yourself plenty of writing room also gives you a feeling of greater freedom, allowing your thoughts to flow uninhibited.

◆ Keep your reader in focus. What information do you wish to convey to them? What's the best approach for reaching them? Speak to them in their language. Tell them your central purpose at the beginning and, if it's a lengthy report, explain to them how it is organised.

◆ Omit needless words. Be concise. Trimming the excess fat from your writing allows the key points to stand out. After writing a letter or report, go back over it and delete any unnecessary words or sentences. It will do wonders for your style.

◆ Keep it simple. Write to express rather than impress. Use short sentences, paragraphs and words. Double talk may have gotten you good grades in high-school English, but it isn't the clearest way to communicate. Each sentence should contain one thought, and each paragraph should be built around a topic sentence that expresses the overall thought of the paragraph. Usually, though not always, the first sentence is the topic sentence.

◆ Avoid ambiguous words. Certainly all words are to some degree ambiguous. However, some are more so than others. Writing is one-way communication where the reader isn't always present to ask the writer to clarify what is meant. We have all received written communications which have defied understanding. Some were just badly written, while others clearly demonstrated that the main object of the exercise was to show off the writer's extensive vocabulary.

◆ Back up your general thoughts with specific facts, ideas or illustrations. The best writing is that which is specific and definite enough to hold the reader's interest. Good writing brings pictures to the reader's mind by presenting definite illustrations.

◆ Write in a style that is natural to you. Writing is nothing more than projecting your thoughts on paper. Write the way you speak and your message will more frequently come across. Don't write 'The boss was subsequently terminated from his position.' Write 'The boss was fired.' Don't write 'I have found osculatory experiences to be a most pleasurable sensation.' Write 'I like kissing.' When we write as we speak, our style tends to be vigorous, crisp and active.

◆ Never underestimate your reader's intelligence or overestimate their knowledge. It's one thing to write in a simple, direct style and another to write down to your reader.

Volumes have been written on the subject of writing and I suggest you seek out one of those for more information. Improving your writing effectiveness involves organisation, simplification and practice.

IMPROVING YOUR READING EFFECTIVENESS

The printed word is here to stay and getting stronger every day. We hear a lot about how children don't read any more because they prefer to watch television. But if people don't read as children, they are likely to get plenty of on-the-job training later.

Occupations, professions and environments are in such a state of continuous change that people who fail to read put themselves in a poor competitive position. I have never known any highly successful business or professional person who wasn't an avid reader. It's one characteristic common to every effective person I've known.

Effective people have long since learned that knowledge is power. They are also aware that, to remain effective, they must keep themselves informed of the changes and events taking place in the world and in their industry or profession, and adapt as necessary.

Obviously, the problem doesn't lie in finding something to read. This is the age of information overload. There is too little time and too much printed matter vying for our attention. The most important key to reading effectiveness can be summed up in one word — selectivity. Effectiveness in reading, like everything else, consists of doing less better, rather than doing more or doing it faster. If you read at an average rate of 250 words a minute, then knowing *not* to read that 100 000-word book that a friend recommended will save you six hours and 40 minutes of reading time. Through selective reading techniques, you can skim the book and make a fairly rapid decision on whether or not to read it, or what parts to read, Here's how:

◆ Always evaluate your professional reading in light of your goals. Before reading something, ask yourself, 'Is this likely to move me towards my goals?' If not, throw it out or send it on its way.

◆ Look for logic, ideas and major points in reading material. Read the topic sentences of each paragraph. If there is nothing of interest, jump to the next paragraph. If you are looking at a book, scan the information on the jacket, the table of contents, the preface, the index and the author's credentials. You can quickly size up whether there is anything of interest to you or not. If you see only one section or chapter that is of interest, read it and then put the book aside.

◆ Reduce your reading load to the bare necessities. If you subscribe to professional or trade journals, cancel your subscriptions to all but the essential ones. A lot of reading can be delegated to subordinates if you need to keep informed and don't have enough reading time. They in turn can highlight key points or summarise articles for you, thus keeping you and themselves informed.

◆ If you read a book or report that you will have to refer to again, highlight the main points and make notes in the margin. Use Post-it notes to tag important pages. When you have to refer to it later, your rereading time will be much reduced. In addition, being an active reader enhances your ability to remember key ideas.

◆ Don't allow your reading to build up. Resolve to either read something by a certain date or discard it. Keeping informed doesn't mean reading last year's or last month's ideas today.

◆ Finally, you can increase your reading effectiveness by increasing your reading speed, although this isn't nearly as important as being selective. Speed-reading courses claim to reduce reading time in the same way that microwave ovens reduce cooking time. Most people who claim to read at thousands of words a minute are actually only skimming the text. Their ability to understand and retain what they read for a sustained period of time is somewhat impaired. Nevertheless, most speed-reading courses will significantly improve your reading ability.

Some of the techniques taught in speed-reading courses are things you can practise on your own. For example, take in a phrase at a time rather than a word at a time. Force yourself to scan more rapidly and take in larger eyefuls. Don't reread, just keep pressing on. It may seem awkward at first, but eventually your reading speed will increase.

Accepting the challenge to reduce paper work can enhance everyone's effectiveness. Generate as little paper as possible and arrange to shield yourself from all paper except that which is absolutely necessary. Be selective. Create positive habits for dealing with paper, and increase your effectiveness with improved reading and writing skills. As long as you're in the midst of the paper war, you'll never find yourself a place in the sun.

REMEMBER

Resolve to make every day count.

Be decisive and have the courage to act.

Procrastination, interruptions
and drop-in visitors are all costly –
try and keep them under control.

Meetings are costly, eliminate
useless meetings and make the ones
you can't avoid more effective.

PART 4

WORKING

WITH

YOUR TEAM

CHAPTER 9

WHO ELSE CAN DO THE JOB?

*By working faithfully eight hours a day
you may eventually get to be a boss
and work twelve hours a day.*

ROBERT FROST

Do you work long hours or find yourself taking work home? Do you find yourself doing routine jobs others could do or be trained to do? Do you have trouble completing important tasks on schedule because you are doing your job as well as someone else's? If you answered yes to any of these questions, then you are a likely victim of the do-it-yourself work tapes discussed in Chapter 1.

As I pointed out earlier, there simply isn't enough time in one lifetime to do everything. However, there is enough time available to get everything done if you use the time of others. Such is the nature of delegation: assigning to others tasks you want or need to get done.

In one sense, delegation is a cornerstone of urban living. We leave it to others to provide our transportation, to grow and prepare our food, build and furnish our homes, educate our children and so on. How many people made it possible for you to obtain this book? I'm sure at least a few hundred. The same is true for your food, car and clothing. We learned long ago that assigning jobs to specialists makes for a society that works less and accomplishes more.

Yet, in our jobs and daily lives many of us don't use delegation to best advantage. We perform many tasks whose completion is of little or no importance. Or we spend our time on jobs that could be more effectively done by others. As a result, less time is spent on the high-priority tasks that only we can carry out effectively. Our effectiveness is thus severely diluted.

The history of delegation is documented as far back as the Book of Exodus in the Old Testament. After leading his people out of Egypt, Moses became a victim of the do-it-yourself myth. He insisted on personally deciding every controversy that arose among the people of Israel. His father-in-law, Jethro, realised that Moses was suffering from a bad case of overcommitment and recommended a plan which would enable Moses to be more effective. First, educate the people in the law; and second, choose able people to deal with routine matters. This would free Moses to concentrate his time and energy on more important, long-range and non-routine matters of governing. Thus, the Scripture states:

> Moses hearkened to the voice of his father-in-law and did all that he had said. And Moses chose able men out of all Israel, and made them heads over the people, rulers of thousands, rulers of hundreds, rulers of fifties, and rulers of tens. And they judged the people at all seasons; the hard causes they brought unto Moses, but every small matter they judged themselves.

So one of the most important people in history became even more effective through delegation. Of course, we have to take into account the fact that Moses had the original to-do and not-to-do list. And he didn't waste any paper either.

The ability to skilfully delegate tasks is one of the keys to success. Knowing what to do and what to assign is important for everyone, even those who don't have others working directly for them. We can all profit from delegation, be it at home or at work.

WHY DO MOST OF US DELEGATE LESS THAN WE SHOULD?

It Doesn't Occur to Us to Delegate

We are often so caught up in the act of doing something, that it simply doesn't occur to us to get someone else to do it. There might be many jobs at home or at work that others could be doing, but out of habit we simply go ahead and perform them. There is a simple antidote for this. Whenever you have a task to complete, ask yourself, 'Can someone else do this?' If so, then get someone else to do it. Find someone else to cut your lawn or screen your mail and sort out the salient points for you. This practice gives you more time and energy to allocate to tasks with the highest payoffs. It may cost you a few dollars to get your lawn cut, but you can use the time saved to embark on a creative project or business deal that could earn you an unlimited amount of money. Time spent in creatively developing one good idea has a payoff far greater than fixing the toaster, cutting the lawn or going through piles of mail. Whenever you can afford it, take advantage of professional services so that you are free to do the things you enjoy most.

We Believe it's a Sign of Weakness

This irrational idea is probably a throwback to early childhood. As infants we come into the world totally helpless. Our lives are in a state of total delegation, and our survival depends on others performing tasks for us. As we mature, the parental message to us is, 'Grow up, be strong and learn to take care of yourself. Grown-ups can do for themselves and babies can't.' Like many outdated tapes, this one plays on into our adult life.

The image of the totally self-sufficient person may have been valid in an earlier rural society, but in 20th century urban society it is a myth. As was pointed out earlier, we are all dependent on each other for our food, clothing, housing, protection and practically everything else in our present society. To delegate is anything but a sign of weakness. However, *not* to delegate is to undervalue your most valuable resource, time.

We Believe it's Immoral

This concept is a by-product of the work tapes. The reasoning goes something like this: 'If we aren't doing anything tangible, then we aren't working hard, and everyone knows and believes in the virtues of hard work. Therefore, by delegating tasks, we fail to work hard and thus lead an immoral life.'

All morality is based on two very simple principles: don't hurt yourself, and don't hurt anyone else. If there is a way that delegation necessarily has to violate either of those principles, I fail to see it.

We Want to Do the Job Ourselves

Many of us fill up our days performing trivial tasks that could easily be delegated. The reason given is usually, 'So what? I enjoy it.' However, the 'enjoyment' gained by doing less important jobs is often a way of avoiding tackling more important ones that we know less about or that seem less pleasant. It gives us a feeling of accomplishment and quells any guilt or insecurity we feel about ignoring important tasks.

Tony, an aeronautical engineer, is a classic example. Because of his technical competence and performance, Tony was promoted to a managerial position. Unfortunately, he refused to carry out his new managerial tasks and insisted on spending his time on comfortable and familiar tasks. Within two weeks of moving into his new office, Tony had his old drawing board moved in. There he spent his days doing exactly what he had been working on in his old job and neglecting his supervisory responsibilities. As expected, administrative problems piled up and Tony escaped each day at the drawing board, refusing to delegate his design work to engineers. Ultimately, he resigned and went to work as an engineer at a competing firm. Although he was bright, competent and a good worker, Tony was his own worst enemy.

We Fear Losing Control

Insecure managers are a common target for this delegation phobia. Such people fear that if subordinates are trained to perform more duties, they will lose their job to one of them.

Like most fears, the fear of losing control is without any real basis and merely holds us back from developing our true potential. If you play such games, sooner or later people will wise up to the fact and start to question whether they need you.

'I'm too busy to delegate'

In many situations, delegation does take time — time to assign the job, sometimes to train the person and to check to see that the job is done satisfactorily. Like planning, delegating is initially time-consuming but in the final analysis it's a time- and energy-saver. Being too busy to delegate is like being too busy to plan. By not making the initial investment of time, you only increase your chances of becoming an ineffective wheel spinner.

'I can do it better and faster myself'

Once again, the problem here is expediency in the short run at the expense of long-range effectiveness. By doing the job yourself, you are only ensuring that you will have to do it again in future. This excuse also fails to take into account the need to develop the potential of others. This is important, particularly if you are leading an organisation, be it a family, a department, a corporation or a religious group. If you hold a position of authority, one of your duties is to train others to be useful and productive members. By neglecting to delegate, you block their opportunity to learn and grow by doing.

'My boss won't let me delegate'

Your boss might insist that you personally attend to certain tasks rather than delegate them. For example, if you are a department manager, your boss might insist that you personally interview and recruit all of your employees rather than delegate the job to an assistant or the personnel department. Or if you stay at home to care for the children, your partner might expect you to also do all the housework rather than hire a part-time cleaner. In either situation the problem is the same: there is a misunderstanding over the most important aspects of your job.

If you can convince your boss that delegating will bring better results, then the problem is well on its way to being resolved. Perhaps you can convince your boss to let you try delegating a task for a trial period and see what happens. If the results are favourable, you can continue to delegate; if they are unfavourable, your boss may have been right all along — it may be an important task that only you should do.

We Fear Being Disliked

Most of us will not admit to it, but the fear of being disliked by our subordinates is a very potent reason for not delegating. Fear strikes out when reality is the pitcher. The fact is, most people like to feel that they are valued by the organisations to which they belong. To make a contribution, they must be given something meaningful to do. By not delegating anything to them, you hinder their ability to make a greater contribution. Subordinates usually look upon skilful delegators much more favourably than they do those who insist on doing everything themselves.

We Fear Making Mistakes and Being Criticised

Perfectionism can be a ticket to ineffectiveness. Very often the problem lies with someone who will not tolerate any mistakes and thus is afraid to delegate. 'If I assign this job to Peter, he won't do it without messing it up' and 'They won't do it my way' are common rationalisations of the perfectionist.

Another cause of perfectionism is when your boss or organisation won't tolerate mistakes. A work climate where no one has the right to be wrong is one that stifles growth and effectiveness. When people are criticised for making mistakes, they soon learn that they can't be wrong if they don't do anything. Consequently, they do as little as possible in order to avoid making mistakes.

Delegatees Don't Want to Accept Responsibility

You assign someone a job and bingo, they drop it right back in your lap. Such a practice is called reverse delegation. You often find this if you try to delegate tasks in an intolerant work environment.

Joe, a mechanic, was a chronic reverse delegator. Joe had been with the same automobile dealership for almost 15 years and was said by his supervisor to be one of his best technicians. However, whenever Joe was assigned an engine to work on, he insisted on okaying every detail of the job with his supervisor.

A new supervisor came on the job and tried to encourage Joe to make decisions and be more autonomous. However, Joe would always reply, 'You're the boss. I just work here and don't want any responsibility.' When I asked Joe why he didn't want to take any responsibility, his answer was: 'Because when I'm right no one remembers, and when I'm wrong no one forgets.'

'No one else has the experience or competence'

If your assistants or employees are incompetent, what are you paying them for? Even if you can't get rid of them, you still may be able to get someone else to do the job. Most of us tend to underrate what our spouse, children, colleagues or subordinates can do. The only way to find out is to give them the ball and let them run with it. It's also the only way they will get the necessary experience to become competent.

Doing Everything Ourselves Makes Us Feel Indispensable

Often our need to be needed is what stands between us and effectiveness. Doing everything yourself doesn't make you indispensable. The simple fact is that nothing will make you indispensable, because no one is. Life was going on for centuries before you were born and will continue, we hope, for centuries after. If you are trying to prove you are indispensable, be honest with yourself and stop indulging your ego. It's to your own benefit to accept reality rather than hide from it.

We Want All the Credit All the Time

In today's competitive work place it's not uncommon for managers who are driven by the desire to reach the top, to do everything themselves. They fear that if those to whom they delegate succeed in a project, the credit will go to them instead of the manager and thus lessen the manager's chance of promotion. It's always helpful to ask ourselves this question: 'If I can't get my subordinates promoted, should I be promoted?'

We Want the Admiration, Respect or Pity of Others

By doing everything ourselves, we prove to our friends, relatives, subordinates and colleagues what a hard-working, totally dedicated person we are. Unwillingness to delegate is a common trait among harried workers. By not delegating, they present themselves with an impossible workload. The sympathy that this evokes is just what they want. This is an unhealthy ego trip, as well as a great excuse for poor work.

We Don't Understand the Situation

What is needed here is more information to familiarise you with the problem. Usually more information will give you enough insight to know who to ask for help.

STRATEGIES FOR DELEGATING EFFECTIVELY

The following ideas will help you to make better use of your opportunities to delegate.

◆ Give the job to the person or organisation that can do it best. Select the right person or persons and the battle is 80 per cent won. In an employment situation, we often confuse the best person for the job with the person who comes at the highest price. While it is true that you will often have to pay top dollars for an excellent job, paying top dollars doesn't guarantee you will get the right person.

A good example of this are the major football league competitions. Year after year, certain teams finish high in the standings and some are considered dynasties. The secret is simple. The coaches and scouts have the ability to pick winning players consistently. On the other hand, consistently losing teams have been known to spend small fortunes on talent, only to end up with the same poor results.

Andrew Carnegie, the American industrialist who was rather good at procuring gold, put it this way: 'Take away my factories, my trade, my avenue of transportation, my money, but leave me my people and in four years, I will have re-established myself.'

Most coaches will tell you that the most important factor in winning is recruiting. Whether you are coaching a team or running a business, the situation is the same in that you are getting things done through others. And the cardinal rule of delegation is that you can't expect winning results with losing players.

◆ Ensure that those who are doing the task have the right training and tools. I touched on the need for proper tools in Chapter 3. Obviously, if you are giving the job to others, it is now they who need the training and tools.

◆ Take special care to clearly and accurately communicate the nature and scope of your delegation. If you don't take time to explain what you expect, or if your delegatee doesn't ask, then chances are that you are both in for rough sailing. This is, of course, assuming that the delegatee hasn't done the job before.

◆ Give credit to those who do the job. Sincere recognition for a job well done will increase your effectiveness in working through others. A former boss of mine once told me, 'It's amazing what you can get done when you are willing to give someone else credit. All I do is hire people who are smarter than me, then I explain what I want done and then recognise them for the outstanding job they do.'

Make the effort to recognise and give credit to someone who does good work. Recognising and rewarding desirable behaviour greatly increases the likelihood that it will be repeated in the future.

◆ Help others to work less and accomplish more. Giving people meaningless tasks is one sure way to put them off-side and lower their willingness to co-operate.

When you assign someone a task, make it worthy of their time and effort. Like you, they value their time and energy. Provide the support necessary to get the job done in the easiest way without sacrificing quality. Such an approach increases your chances of succeeding as a delegator.

◆ Put an end to reverse delegation. When you assign someone a task, there is no reason it has to come back to you like a boomerang. If you tolerate reverse delegation, then you aren't really delegating. When someone drops a problem back in your lap, tell them, 'I gave you the job to do because I wanted to see how you would handle it.' If they still wish to discuss matters with you, ask them to think of as many solutions to the problem as they can, put them in writing and choose what they believe is the best one. This will increase their decision making skill and reduce the time you spend consulting with them. When they have formulated solutions to the problem, you then have the basis for an effective discussion.

◆ Delegate the right to be different and wrong. Just because someone doesn't do the job your way doesn't mean they are any less capable. We would consider a coach odd, at best, if they insisted that a left-handed tennis player use their right hand because the coach is right-handed. Yet how often do we insist that others do things our way?

Similarly, mistakes are a part of the learning process and should be expected and tolerated as long as people are willing to learn from them. I once heard of a manager who made his employees stand and admit to at least one mistake they had made that week. The manager reasoned that those who didn't have any mistakes to report probably weren't willing to be innovative. It's an interesting thought. Life is, in one sense, a process of mistakes. I personally believe that it's better to have people discuss their successes and to quietly tolerate intelligent mistakes.

◆ Realise that delegation doesn't free you from responsibility. A classic illustration of this was the sign on former US president Harry Truman's desk saying, 'The buck stops here.' Even though you assign a job to someone else, you don't transfer your responsibility for seeing that the job gets done.

◆ Assign tasks by requesting rather than ordering. We live in a free society where everyone has a choice. Others can do the job you want them to do, or tell you to go do it yourself. All of us like to think of ourselves as worthy of respect and courtesy. Consequently, how you go about assigning tasks is often as important as what you assign. There's a great deal of difference between saying, 'Debbie, can you wrap up the Hobart report this week?' and 'Debbie, wrap up the Hobart report this week.' It may not make any difference to whether or not the report gets done, but the cumulative effect of behaving like an autocrat is sooner or later bound to take its toll. Resort to giving orders only when everything else fails. Courtesy and respect are contagious. In delegating, a little tact goes a long way.

◆ Specify the conditions for satisfactory performance at the outset. Have you ever given someone a job to do, only to remark later, 'This isn't what I wanted at all'? This can usually be avoided by taking the time to explain what you want done, how you want it done and when you want it done. It may also help to specify subgoals or request progress reports on long-term assignments.

In addition to communicating your expectations, it is useful to explain why the task is necessary. Often the reasons for doing a job are not apparent to the person who has to do it. If you take the time to explain a job's importance, people will usually be better motivated.

◆ Follow up. As long as you are responsible for a task, it's your job to ensure that it is carried out. Thus, the final step in most delegation is to check on the performance of the delegatee. Habitually delegating without following up invites problems. Follow-up questions to ask are: 'Who did the job?' 'How was it done?' 'Was the work satisfactory?' 'What can be done to do the job faster, more easily and better in the future?'

These are the basic ingredients for successful delegation. Skilful delegation will give you more time to devote to tasks that only you can carry out successfully, or to other areas of your life. It can also improve your relationships with others. Such a small initial investment of time can give you a great payoff.

HOW YOUR ASSISTANT CAN HELP YOU TO WORK LESS AND ACCOMPLISH MORE

A discussion of delegation wouldn't be complete without at least touching on the subject of personal assistants. If you talk to successful people, they are often quick to attribute much of their success to their administrative assistants. Competent, trustworthy assistants are worth their weight in gold.

The following is a list of things your personal assistant can do to enable you to increase your effectiveness:

◆ Learn your principles of organisation and see to it that you stay organised. They can keep your desk clear and see to it that the highest priority item on your to-do list is waiting on your desk first thing each morning.

◆ Handle routine correspondence and decision making. You can draft answers to routine queries received in your office as models for your assistant to follow. This frees you to work on non-routine and non-recurring types of problems.

◆ Keep your appointment schedule and act as a buffer to screen you from drop-in visitors and telephone calls, leaving you to work uninterrupted on important matters.

◆ Reduce your reading time by screening your mail and highlighting items worthy of your attention.

◆ Provide valuable assistance in the substantive part of your work by suggesting solutions to problems. If you are charged with writing a research report or preparing a budget, your assistant could locate and gather the necessary information and digest it into a meaningful form ready for your use. And as a sounding board for your ideas, an assistant can keep you sharp by helping you to identify any potential pitfalls or substantial oversights.

◆ Serve as a goodwill ambassador to all who come in contact with your office.

Guidelines for Increasing the Effectiveness of Assistants

Personal assistants are in a powerful position. A good and dedicated assistant can compensate for many of your shortcomings, and a poor or unmotivated one can greatly reduce your effectiveness. With that in mind, here are some thoughts to help you get the most from working with your assistant:

◆ Get the very best one you can. Don't hire someone to take dictation, file and type. Get an alert, bright, educated person who is worthy of your time and trust. Look for a diamond in the rough. Often you will spot a talented, ambitious person whose only shortcoming is lack of training in management skills. You might consider hiring such a person and paying the cost of training them. Business schools and universities have recognised the need for training people in management as well as clerical skills.

◆ Your assistant is a key member of your team. Never underestimate the power of a good assistant.

◆ Keep your assistant informed of your goals, priorities and aspirations. This will enable them to organise your work for greatest effectiveness. Ask for ideas. Many senior executives reach the top because they have been smart enough to listen to and act on the suggestions of their assistants. Consider you and your assistant as a team.

◆ Don't waste your assistant's time by putting them on hold while you fumble around for documents, addresses or telephone numbers. Such habits, along with assigning needless tasks, are great ways to alienate a valuable member of your team.

◆ Give your assistant the authority to make decisions and solve problems. If they haven't been given such authority before, start with small, routine tasks, then gradually turn over more complex assignments. You will be pleasantly surprised at what gets done.

◆ Give your assistant all the support, recognition, respect and salary you can. According to an anonymous source, an assistant should have the following qualifications: 'A diplomat's tact, a mule's endurance, a chameleon's effacement, a salesman's enthusiasm, the sun's punctuality, the speed of light, a sister's loyalty, a rhino's hide, an Einsteinian brain, a mother's sympathy and the patience of Job.'

Anyone who has a first-class assistant will likely tell you that this is an understatement.

CHAPTER 10

KEEPING COMMUNICATIONS OPEN

It takes two to tango.
PROVERB

COMMUNICATION IS THE weak link in the chain of working with others. In the past century, we have made superhuman technical advances in our ability to communicate rapidly and with more people. We live in a society in which we are continually bombarded by information. Yet while more and more messages are being passed, it appears that our ability to convey what we actually mean hasn't improved. The infinite capacity of people to misunderstand each other makes our jobs and our lives far more difficult than they need be.

Although the problem of communication breakdowns will never be completely solved, the situation isn't totally hopeless either. Most of us do little to improve our ability to understand and be understood, because we simply take communication for granted. Most people assume that they are good communicators and place the burden of understanding on others.

With an understanding of the basic concepts of communication, we can begin to see some of the common ways in which faulty communication occurs. The first step towards resolving any type of problem is to recognise it. So, the first step towards understanding poor communication is to realise that . . .

AS WE PERCEIVE, SO DO WE COMMUNICATE

Our ability to communicate is interwoven with our perceptions and thought processes. Someone may tell you, 'I know just how you feel', but no one knows how anyone else actually feels because no two people experience the exact same things. Your experiences, your sensory devices and your ability to think are uniquely yours. It is this tremendous difference in experience and perception that greatly hinders our ability to communicate.

Our ability to perceive is also governed by our needs. People generally see what they want to see. If you believe that the person you are speaking to is hostile, friendly or dull, then you will tend to see them that way. When we meet someone we perceive as important, we tend to overestimate their height. Thus our ability to accurately perceive reality is greatly distorted by our needs.

In addition to being limited by our experiences and perceptive abilities, our ability to communicate is affected by the way we encode or decode meanings into symbols. The fact is that what we experience cannot be transmitted as experience, but rather must be symbolically communicated.

Any type of communication involves a symbolic process. Something else must stand for what we are really trying to get across. Someone buys a Rolls-Royce and parks it in his driveway as a symbol of wealth. Another person frowns to symbolise his displeasure. Still a third says 'I love you' to someone to symbolise his affection for them. As a small child you may have learned the expression 'Sticks and stones may break my bones, but words can never hurt me.' All this tells us is that words are merely symbols that, in themselves, are harmless. Yet do we really react to words as though they are mere symbols?

The Intensional Orientation

If I were to blindfold you, put cold spaghetti in your mouth and convince you that I was feeding you worms, you would probably become ill. However, it isn't the real world but rather the verbal world that would cause your discomfort. However, if you realised that all I was giving you was cold spaghetti, it probably wouldn't matter much what I said. In the first case, you would be behaving intensionally by reacting to the verbal world as if it were the real world. In the second case, you would check your experience with your taste buds; this is known as behaving extensionally.

The intensional orientation can cause us to waste time and energy on matters that exist only in the mind. Relying on symbolic maps without checking out the territory can cause us a great deal of unnecessary concern.

The following fable provides an excellent example of how behaving intensionally can affect a business.

> A man lived by the side of the road and sold hot dogs. He had no radio. He had trouble with his eyes, so he had no newspaper. But he sold good hot dogs. He put up a sign on the highway, saying how good they were. He stood by the side of the road and cried: 'Buy a hot dog, mister,' and people bought. He increased his meat and bun orders, and he bought a bigger store to take care of his trade. He got his son home from college to help him. But then something happened. His son said: 'Father, haven't you been listening to the radio? There's a big depression on. The international situation is terrible, and the domestic situation is even worse.' Whereupon his father thought: 'Well, my son has been to college. He listens to the radio and reads the papers, so he ought to know.' So, the father cut down his bun order, took down his advertising sign, and no longer bothered to stand on the highway to sell hot dogs. His hot-dog sales fell almost overnight. 'You were right son,' the father said to the boy. 'We are certainly in the middle of a great depression.

The One-word One-definition Fallacy

This is another cause of communication going astray. In Lewis Carroll's *Through the Looking-Glass*, Humpty Dumpty arrogantly says to Alice, 'When I use a word, it means just what I choose it to mean, neither more nor less.' When it comes to communicating, most of us operate much like Humpty Dumpty. The implicit assumption is that words mean the same thing to the other party as they do to us. Yet for the 500 most commonly used English words, there are over 14 000 dictionary definitions. It's easy to see why very often the words may come through, but the meaning doesn't.

Much of our humour, both intentional and unintentional, is derived from the multiple meanings of words. For example, consider the sign hanging in a dry-cleaning establishment which reads, 'Drop your pants here — you will receive prompt attention.' Or consider these attempts by motorists to describe to their insurance companies the events that led to an accident:

- ◆ Coming home, I drove into the wrong house and collided with a tree I don't have.
- ◆ I collided with a stationary truck coming the other way.
- ◆ A pedestrian hit me and went under my car.
- ◆ The guy was all over the road. I had to swerve a number of times before I hit him.
- ◆ In my attempt to kill a fly, I drove into a telephone pole.
- ◆ I had been driving my car for 40 years when I fell asleep at the wheel and had an accident.
- ◆ I was on my way to the doctor's with rear end trouble when my universal joint gave way, causing me to have an accident.
- ◆ An invisible car came out of nowhere, struck my vehicle and vanished.
- ◆ The pedestrian had no idea which direction to go, so I ran over him.
- ◆ The telephone pole was approaching fast. I was attempting to swerve out of its path when it struck my front end.

When you stop and think about it, no word has exactly the same meaning to any two people. Words have multiple meanings. Word definitions change over time. Different regions use different words to describe the same things. Every word conjures up a different thought in someone's mind. When you become aware of the inadequacy of words, you start to wonder how anyone ever manages to communicate anything meaningfully.

THE EITHER–OR TRAP

This is a problem when the structure of language lulls us into erroneous thinking. Consider the following statements:

◆ Helena is either in her twenties of her thirties.
◆ David is either an Australian citizen or he isn't.
◆ Bruce either graduated from university or he didn't.

Now consider the following additional statements:

◆ Helena is either intelligent or stupid.
◆ David is either honest or dishonest.
◆ Bruce is either competent or incompetent.

The first set of statements are legitimate dichotomies and the second set are false dichotomies. All of the first statements are valid depictions of reality, but what about the second set? The answers to those statements can't really be verified in simple yes–no, either–or, black–white terms. It's a matter of degree.

Unfortunately, the structure of our language makes no distinction between true and false dichotomies. Hence we often tend to think in simplistic terms, such as rich–poor, sick–healthy, good–evil, beautiful–ugly, smart–dumb, true–false, right–wrong, guilty–innocent, war–peace, success–failure and so on. The vast middle ground where reality usually lies is completely ignored.

Throughout our lives, we are constantly conditioned to polarise our thinking. At school, you learned that there were right answers to questions, and that all other answers were wrong. In competitive sports, there is a winner and a loser. The courts decree a defendant guilty or not guilty. And let's not forget the all-time favourite — there are two sides to every story. Unfortunately, either–or thinking seems to be more the rule than the exception in our society.

The I've-said-it-all Myth

Bertrand Russell, the English philosopher, once remarked, 'The demand for certainty is one that is natural to man, but is nevertheless an intellectual vice.' All too often we speak with the unconscious assumption that we are totally correct and that whatever we utter has thoroughly covered the subject. The next time you see two people engaged in a heated argument, notice the absolute authority with which they speak.

Of course, the fact is that it's impossible to say everything about anything. As was pointed out earlier, communicating means necessarily abstracting, and abstracting means that certain things will be left out. Yet with our own limited perceptions and abstractions, we try to convince others of how absolutely correct we are.

Confusing Our Inferences with Reality

This is another pattern in which faulty thinking results in poor communication. Consider the following hypothetical example. You are driving your car and are stopped at a stop sign at a busy intersection. On your left you see a car approaching with its left blinker on. You assume the driver is turning, so you start to cross the intersection and bang! You hit him broadside. Later you learn that his blinker was on because he planned to turn into his driveway, which was 30 metres past the intersection.

Let's retrace your thought processes that led up to the accident. First, you received a message in the form of a turn signal. Then you inferred that the signal meant the other driver would turn at the intersection. You made this inference totally unaware that you were making one and proceeded to act on the inference as if it were reality. Consequently, you crossed the intersection and paid the price.

We can't avoid inferences and we make hundreds of them every day. The problems begin when we make them without recognising that we are doing so. The consequences of such a mistake can range from humorous to fatal. Unfortunately, the nature of our language doesn't force us to distinguish between statements of inference and statements of observation. All too often we jump to erroneous conclusions on the basis of vague or incomplete information.

Labels and Stereotypes

Labels and stereotypes constitute another communication mishap that leads us astray. Everyone stereotypes, but no one likes to be stereotyped. And once we pigeonhole someone, or get pigeonholed, the evaluation, however false, tends to stick.

Our culture and educational system teach us to label others and reduce them to stereotypes. Grouping people and things according to similarities can have positive value. However, to be conscious only of similarities is to neglect the differences that exist in all of us. Try this quick exercise.

1. Write down the following things:
your sex, age, race, ethnic background, religion,
educational qualifications, occupation,
marital status, political affiliation, whether you come
from the city or the country, your height and your weight,
whether you went to a state or private school.

**2. Now consider the stereotypes
that are often attributed to these traits.
Do they apply to you?**

To summarise, stereotyping, unawareness of our inferences, the belief in and craving for total certainty, either–or thinking, the one-word one-meaning fallacy, and confusing symbols with the reality they represent are some of the common ways in which communication breaks down. Add to this the fact that most of us blame each other for communication failures and it becomes obvious why misunderstandings are so prevalent.

STRATEGIES THAT WILL MAKE YOU A BETTER COMMUNICATOR

None of us are perfect communicators, but some of us are further from perfection than others. Even if you were a perfect communicator (whatever that might be), you would still find yourself beset with communication problems because you would have to deal with imperfect communicators. The following guidelines will help to make you a more effective communicator.

◆ Recognise the inadequacy of communication. By taking communication for granted, we only increase the chances of greater misunderstanding. Communication seems so simple because we have been doing it for longer than we can remember. However, doing it for a long time and doing it well are not the same thing. It's a complicated symbolic, abstract process with an unlimited number of things that can go wrong — and usually do.

Communication may appear inadequate, but what's our choice? For better or worse, it's all we've got. We simply have to be content with it while recognising that none of us will ever be totally understood.

◆ Become extensional in your thinking. Remember that words are only symbols for reality, in much the same way that maps represent territories. Things are often not what they appear to be.

◆ Listen and look for the total meaning when speaking with someone. Don't just listen for the words. They may not mean the same to you as they do to the other person. Look for gestures, expressions, the sender's posture and tone of voice. Likewise, be conscious of these things when you are the sender. Remember that it's not what you say but how you say it that really communicates your meaning.

◆ Consider the source. Whenever you are evaluating a message, who said it is usually at least as important as what is said. The better you know the communicator, the more accurately you will be able to assess the message and their motive for sending it.

This sounds like an obvious recommendation, but it is one that is often ignored. For example, a colleague may openly criticise your work, when the actual problem is that he feels your potential success will make him look bad. The local computer or photocopier sales representative may tell you that you need their latest hardware when your present machines have you drowning in clutter and information overload. Or your stockbroker may call you incessantly with hot tips. Why shouldn't she? Her commission is based on transactions. It's a good rule of thumb to remember that people will tend to tell you what they want you to hear. And what they want you to hear isn't always in your own best interest.

◆ Tailor your message to your audience. Choose words, concepts and ideas that they can relate to based on their background and knowledge. How well you do this is fundamental to getting your message across.

◆ Ask questions. Many of us are reluctant to ask questions of someone when we aren't sure what the person means. This is usually
borne out of a fear of appearing stupid. However, a lot of confusion
can be avoided by simply asking someone to repeat or rephrase
their statement. If you think you understand but want to be sure,
paraphrase the message and let the sender verify that you do in fact
understand their point. If someone refuses to answer intelligent
questions, they may not be certain of what they are saying. Which
brings us to our next recommendation . . .

◆ Know what you're talking about. Many people pass comments on,
or make judgments about, things they know nothing about.
Someone participating in a recent national poll was asked, 'What
do you think about cyclamates?' Their response was, 'I think any
two cyclamates who live together should get married.'

   You can save yourself and others a lot of future headaches by
taking the time to get your facts straight and know something
about what you are communicating about.

◆ Be specific. Don't beat around the bush by speaking in vague gener-
alities. If you make a general statement, have something specific to
illustrate your point. Don't say, 'Andrews is doing a lousy job as divi-
sion sales manager.' Instead, say, 'Andrews' department has had high
turnover, high absenteeism and a poor track record on sales ever
since he took over last year' — and have the facts to back it up.

◆ Communicate in simple, everyday language. Although many
professional and technical terms are work-savers that allow people
to communicate rapidly with one another, a great deal of what we
read in medical, legal, technical and academic documents is little
more than the old professional snow-job game. If you can't dazzle
them with brilliance, baffle them with jargon. Have you ever tried
to read government legislation or the conveyancing documents for
your house? Good luck. The purpose of much jargon is to protect
the interests of experts rather than the consumer.

   Here is something you can have fun with. It's called the 'Systematic
Buzzword Projector' and has been around for some time. It is believed
to have originated in the Royal Canadian Air Force. Consisting of
three columns of words, it is designed to impress and confuse. Just
think of three digits at random (say 6, 9, 5), look up the correspond-
ing words and presto, buzzwords!

COLUMN 1	COLUMN 2	COLUMN 3
1. integrated	1. management	1. options
2. total	2. organisational	2. flexibility
3. systematised	3. monitored	3. capability
4. parallel	4. reciprocal	4. mobility
5. functional	5. digital	5. programming
6. responsive	6. logic	6. concept
7. optical	7. transitional	7. time-phase
8. synchronised	8. incremental	8. projection
9. compatible	9. sixth-generation	9. hardware
10. balanced	10. policy	10. contingency

The only problem with such communication is that it's mostly non-communication. It's only useful for confusing others and impressing the gullible. Intelligent communicators know how to simplify and tailor their message for greatest understanding by the receiver. Just ask yourself, 'What am I really trying to get across?'

◆ Don't be afraid to say 'I don't know'. We know very little about the world in which we live. The amount of knowledge that we don't have is infinitely larger than the amount of knowledge any one person has. Neither you nor I have a corner on the knowledge market. So what's the big deal if someone asks you a question you honestly have no idea how to answer? Faking the answer only compounds the problems of ignorance.

◆ Remember that anything that communicates is communication. A rumpled, smudged letter filled with errors tells you that the writer is less than meticulous. People who fail to take care of their appearance or health tell you something about their self-image. Punctuality communicates. Body language communicates. Tone of voice communicates. And silence communicates. Keep all of these factors in mind. You may be inadvertently sending wrong messages.

◆ Spring the either–or trap. Most things in life don't fall into simple black and white categories. There are many shades of grey in-between. There is a large middle ground between good and bad, honest and dishonest, success and failure. Think in terms of degrees of goodness, honesty, success and so on.

◆ Realise that you can never say everything about anything. Anytime you communicate about anything, no matter how simple, you will leave something out. Bertrand Russell pointed out that our certainty varies inversely with our knowledge. We will never have all the answers. Beware of those who believe they do. It's a sure sign of ignorance.

◆ Give those you communicate with your undivided attention. Most of us can do only one thing well at a time. Shuffling papers, answering the telephone, staring out the window and tapping your pencil communicate a mood of indifference. If you don't want to talk to someone, don't see them. If you do take the time to communicate with someone, give them the interest and attention that you would have them give you. Listen attentively and contribute to the conversation when appropriate.

◆ Don't interrupt the other person. This is a very quick way to put an end to meaningful communication. Your interruption tells the other party, 'Please shut up — what I have to say is far more important!'

◆ Communicate your ideas at the proper place and at the proper time for maximum useful impact. The office Christmas party isn't the place to ask the boss for a raise or to evaluate your assistant's performance. The location and frame of mind that you and the other party are in have a great deal to do with how well your ideas will be received.

◆ Be aware of your inferences when you communicate. Did you personally observe what you are talking or writing about? If not, then to some degree you are dealing with an inference. If this is the case, you will need to assess the likelihood of its being valid. We can't avoid inferences, and we make a countless number of them every day. Life is a gamble. But we often bet on the sure thing that isn't really sure at all. Successful gambling is usually the result of calculated risk-taking. Be aware of your inferences and the likelihood of their validity before you speak.

◆ Refrain from labelling, stereotyping and making sweeping generalisations about individuals or groups. By doing this, you only blind yourself to the uniqueness of each individual and thus hinder your ability to see others as they really are and to communicate effectively with them. Instead, make an effort to discover the uniqueness of each person you communicate with.

The more often you do this, the faster your stereotyped beliefs will tend to disintegrate.

Don't allow common stereotypes to dictate your own behaviour. You don't have to love pasta because you are Italian or noodles because you are Chinese. Neither are you over the hill because you have reached a certain age. It's all a state of mind.

◆ Don't overcommunicate. It's possible to say too much and, as a result, confuse the listener. Saying too much keeps your main points from standing out by surrounding them with excess verbiage. Worse still, overcommunicators are just plain boring. As James Russell Lowell, the American poet, essayist and diplomat, said, 'In general those who have nothing to say contrive to spend the longest time in doing it.'

◆ Realise that face-to-face communication is an ongoing two-way process that is the joint responsibility of both parties. There will always be communication errors, but they can be corrected in a give-and-take exchange. With regard to this, it's helpful to remember that when a message is sent there are at least six different messages present:

— What you mean to say.
— What you actually say.
— What the other person hears.
— What the other person thinks they heard.
— What the other person says.
— What you think the other person says.

◆ Relax. A relaxed, open attitude will make people more receptive to your ideas and willing to share their ideas with you.

In summary, becoming a more effective communicator requires becoming aware of communication problems and making an effort to correct them.

CHAPTER 11

WORKING WITH —NOT AGAINST

When in Rome, live as the Romans do:
when elsewhere, live as they live elsewhere.
ST AMBROSE

IF YOU WANT to work less and accomplish more, keep this simple point in mind: it's easier to work with people than it is to work against them. If we could harness the time and energy that is wasted in needless conflicts between individuals, businesses, governments and nations, the achievements of humanity would increase at least a hundredfold.

Not all conflict is bad or unnecessary. It's something we all experience within ourselves and with others as we mature. Many conflict and stress situations develop us into stronger and better human beings.

As a teenager, you may have felt torn between your need for security and your need to feel free. In your job, you may have experienced a conflict with your boss over what your most important tasks were. Hopefully, it was resolved by an exchange of ideas that enlightened both you and your boss and made both of you better people for it. In your marriage, you may experience a philosophical difference with your spouse over priorities in the family budget or the proper way to rear children. Such conflicts are a normal part of everyday living and their proper resolution can contribute to personal growth.

Unfortunately, a great deal of interpersonal conflict is totally unproductive and an unnecessary waster of time and energy. You may have three degrees, a string of credentials, and an IQ of 190. You may be one who knows the unknowable and can do the undoable. However, if your life is an endless series of personality conflicts, the chances of your achieving success are greatly reduced. And chances are that others will see to it that you have to work extra hard to achieve anything. Let's not have this happen to you.

This is not to say that you can expect to be rewarded strictly on the basis of your personal charm, for you won't. However, it is equally naive to believe that you will be rewarded or recognised strictly on the basis of merit. Just because you can dance well doesn't mean you'll get invited to the ball. All of us are social creatures and we rarely feel neutral about those with whom we work. The fact is that some people are extremely likeable, while others are about as endearing as funnel-web spiders.

CONFLICT-CREATING PERSONALITIES

It is often difficult to tell why one person is fond of another. However, it is usually quite obvious why unpopular people are unpopular.

Here are 12 prevalent personalities that are abrasive and obnoxious. Unfortunately, we all possess some of their traits.

1. THE CRITIC

The world is full of critics. We even pay some of them to tell us what plays and movies to see, books to read and restaurants to visit. We pay others to tell us what's wrong with our golf swing, or our business, or what to do about our neuroses. Professional and constructive critics perform a useful service, as long as they refrain from using their power to exploit others.

The critics I object to are the ones found on every street corner, in every office and often in the home. Unlike the professionals, they will give you their negative opinions on everything, whether you want to hear them or not. To the critic, nothing anyone else does is better than mediocre. If only you hadn't made that stupid mistake, things would be just fine. Critics have 20–20 hindsight, and are about as welcome as a long drought.

Most critics are frustrated doers who fear failure. To examine their own behaviour would be too painful, so they evaluate yours instead. That way they don't have time to do anything else, and you get to profit from their brilliant insights into what's wrong with the world and you. Brendan Behan, the Irish author, said it best: 'Critics are like eunichs in a harem: they know how it's done, they've seen it done every day, but they're unable to do it themselves.'

Sooner or later you get tired of the critics and tell them where to get off. Usually they are offended and blame the conflict on you. After all, they were only trying to help!

2. The Aggressor

Aggressors pursue their goals with all the grace and tact of a wild pig. They will likely be an advocate of the famous Lombardi philosophy: 'Winning isn't everything. It's the only thing.' Thus, they conclude that the key to winning is a series of power sweeps. They are quick to identify themselves with heroes famous for their 'nobody gets in my way' attitude.

Aggressors often have a burning, almost insatiable desire to dominate and control others. Unfortunately for them, their brute-force tactics usually blow up in their face. People are generally reluctant to give power to those who appear threatening or who lust for power. Aggressors accomplish only that which they can get done with force, usually after a great amount of struggle and confrontation with others. They see themselves as conquering heroes with a few battle scars from having fought the good fight. They like to believe that no one pushes them around. Others just see them as an unnecessary annoyance. They haven't yet learned the difference between aggressiveness and assertiveness.

3. The Gossip

'Psst . . . don't tell any one, but So-lin's in trouble with the boss, the Jacksons' marriage is on the rocks, and Ian got that promotion so fast because he and the boss are having an affair. Don't breathe this to a soul. Okay?'

Gossips fancy themselves as the source of information. They know the real story about what happened and will be happy to fill you in if you promise not to tell anyone. The problem is that gossips usually don't know the real story but rather a half-baked rumour that is a product of someone's wishful thinking. As for confidentiality, Benjamin Franklin put it best: 'Three people can keep a secret if two of them are dead.'

Sooner or later, gossips choke on their own grapevine when their information can't be verified or turns out to be untrue. They are branded as untrustworthy, and people become reluctant to share information with them. Gossips find themselves on the outside looking in.

4. The Moralist

Moralists start wars by taking it upon themselves to tell other people how to live their lives. To moralists, we live in a world of absolutes and they know them all. They will tell you what's right, wrong, good, bad, pleasant and unpleasant with an air of complete certainty. And they'll be sure to tell you, whether you ask for their opinion or not.

On the job, moralists are easy to identify. They tell you how to behave, how to dress, how to keep your desk, whom to associate with both on and off the job, and how to do your work. They are so convinced of the righteousness of their convictions that the idea of live and let live is totally alien to them.

Most intelligent people are insulted by moralists. The subtle putdown is, 'You aren't capable of making your own decisions, so I will make them for you.'

5. The Martyr

Martyrs manipulate others by setting themselves up as sacrificial lambs. Like the moralist, the martyr's primary weapon is guilt. The difference is that moralists tell you to feel guilty, whereas martyrs wield guilt in a covert manner. By word or deed, martyrs let you know that they have sacrificed their own needs for your benefit and that you are selfish and inconsiderate if you won't do what they want you to do.

As a hypothetical example of martyrdom in action, let's assume that you and I meet in a bookshop where you happen to be looking at this book and are trying to decide whether or not to buy it. After looking it over, you decide you would rather spend your money on something else, and you put the book back on the shelf. Assuming the role of a martyr, I would look terribly forlorn and say to you, 'That's okay, you don't have to buy it. Forget that I sacrificed the prime of my life to help people like you. Forget that my eyesight has suffered from poring over the manuscript. You just don't understand how tough it is to write a book. Maybe someday when you write a book of your own, you'll know the agony of it all. Then you'll know how it feels to get rejections from publishers and flack from editors. Go ahead and put the book down. Forget about me.'

Of course, in choosing to play the role of a martyr, I left out a few details. First, I wrote the book because I wanted to. Second, I enjoyed writing it. And third, it's a profit-making venture on the part of the publisher and myself.

Despite their cries of sacrifice, martyrs are the most selfish people of all. Few of us can enjoy the benefits of someone else's self-denial. Of course, martyrs aren't really self-sacrificing. They are getting some sort of perverse pleasure from playing the sacrificial-lamb game with you. Once you are aware of their games, you can ignore them. Paying attention to martyrs is a waste of time.

6. THE PERFECTIONIST

Perfectionism and its problems were discussed earlier. Have you ever known anyone who said, 'I'm a perfectionist in everything I do'? Many of us erroneously believe that such a philosophy is the key to effective living.

Perfectionists waste a great deal of their time and energy and, if you aren't careful, they'll waste yours, too. If you work with a perfectionist, you will frequently find yourself spending 90 per cent of your time to get a 1 per cent increase in results. Many people who fancy themselves as perfectionists are wheel-spinners who actually accomplish little or nothing.

7. THE TRIVIA GENERATOR

Trivia generators keep themselves busy by keeping everyone else busy. In fact, busywork for you and them is their only goal. They are the classic victims of the activity-means-productivity myth. No one has ever bothered to tell them that jumping around and splashing in the water doesn't mean they are swimming.

It's tough enough to be effective without the needless harassment of a make-work artist. Consequently, those who create superfluous tasks are very easy to dislike and can create a great deal of needless conflict.

8. THE SHORT FUSE

These people who react excessively and too quickly, without stopping to reflect on the situation they are confronted with. As a result, they often complicate problems or create unnecessary conflicts. To such people, every new problem is one of paramount urgency and importance. They are very highly strung, intense and quick to lose their temper. Because they lack perspective, they spend most of their time solving unnecessary problems that they create for themselves and everyone else. They are quick to jump to conclusions on the basis of insufficient or inaccurate information and pay the high price of being in disharmony with their subordinates, boss, family and friends.

A department manager named Bajia created a great deal of havoc when she decided one day that the clerical staff were taking too long over their coffee breaks. She started spot-checking the coffee breaks and severely reprimanded several clerks for what she termed 'excessive chatter'.

As a result, the clerks got together and started a work-to-rule campaign. Morale in the department soon declined, absenteeism increased and several clerks found jobs elsewhere. A clerical bottleneck was created and it was Bajia's responsibility to solve it. She couldn't, and she was replaced.

9. The Bragger

'Mine is better than yours' is the motto of the bragger, and they take pains to remind you of it at every opportunity. With absolutely no encour-agement, they will tell you about their new flat, their expensive car or their great job. In truth, most braggers believe that theirs isn't as good as yours, so they attempt to impress you by exaggerating their success.

This doesn't mean that you shouldn't have a strong belief in your own abilities, for you are probably better than you give yourself credit for. However, so are other people. People who truly believe in themselves have little need to broadcast it to the world. The only thing most braggers convince other people of is that they have a big mouth and a poor self-image.

10. The Cynic

Cynics always look for the downside. They are the ultimate kill-joy. Do you have a new job? The company cynic will tell you how it has no future. Did you recently buy a new house? The neighbourhood cynic will tell you that the neighbourhood is declining. Are you contemplating marriage or having children? The family cynic will be quick to tell you about all the drudgeries of domesticity. Most cynics are little more than disillusioned idealists.

11. THE PUT-DOWN ARTIST

Put-down artists try to enhance their own stature by belittling others. They haven't yet learned that they are no more or no less a person for what other people do or have. Consequently, their attempts at self-enhancement are carried out at the expense of others. Such behaviour accomplishes nothing except to needlessly waste time.

Put-down artists can be subtle in their approach, and if you aren't careful you might find yourself caught up in one of their games. For example, someone might ask you for advice and then reject all of your suggestions.

Consider the following dialogue between a sales representative and his boss.

Rep: What can I do to increase my sales?

Boss: Have you considered making more calls in your territory?

Rep: Yes, that appears to be a good idea, but it's difficult to make appointments in advance and most customers only see sales-people on certain days of the week.

Boss: Perhaps you could supplement your personal selling with long-distance phone calls.

Rep: I've tried that, but telephone calls don't do the trick. They lack the personal touch of face-to-face contact.

Boss: Have you tried soliciting business through the mail?

Rep: Even though it sounds good, that's the worst suggestion of all. Mail solicitations are seldom answered. Most of them end up in the rubbish bin.

And so it goes: yes, but . . . yes, but . . . yes, but . . . The sales representative doesn't want advice. He's trying to discount the boss.

In another instance, you might be asked to make a decision where you will be damned if you do and damned if you don't.

A special kind of put-down artist is one who puts himself (or herself) down — the kick-me player. They will tell you how stupid or irresponsible they are, and then follow through with inaction to back up their statements. As a result, they get kicked out of their job, out of university or out of their marriage.

More frequently, however, put-down artists aim their arrows of destruction at you and others. If you don't take pains to ignore such people, they can waste a lot of your time and energy in needless bickering.

12. THE CON ARTIST

Although they come in various shapes and sizes, all con artists show one thing — a lack of integrity. They take great pains to deceive others for their own personal benefit.

Such people are easily recognised by their ability to consistently say one thing and do another. Your boss tells you that she always likes to promote from within the firm, but then fills vacant positions with outsiders. A colleague tells you that nothing of consequence is on the agenda for the budget committee's meeting and so there is no need for you to attend. Later you learn that the budget for your pet project has been slashed, and your colleague got extra funding for his. Hypocrisy is the *modus operandi* of the con artist.

Dealing with con artists can be very tricky and time-consuming, especially when you don't recognise them as such. Listed below in the left-hand column are typical statements made by con artists. The right-hand column sets out what they really mean.

WHEN CON ARTISTS SAY:	THEY REALLY MEAN:
1. I'm only trying to help you. Your welfare is all that matters.	1. You look like a real sucker. With a little luck, I can take you for all you're worth.
2. You can't trust anybody but me. It's a jungle out there, but I'll show you the ropes.	2. You'd be better off trusting almost anyone but me. Once we're in the jungle, you'll be at my mercy.
3. The trouble with you is you won't listen. Your stubbornness is going to lead to your undoing.	3. The trouble with you is I can't manipulate you. What are you, intelligent or something?

The way to detect a con artist is to close your ears and open your eyes. Andrew Carnegie, the American industrialist, said, 'As I grow older, I pay less attention to what men say. I just watch what they do.' Such a practice can also keep you from being exploited.

So there you have the disruptive dozen. You will always be plagued by them to some degree. However, by controlling your own behaviour, you can ensure that the disruptive dozen will have a minimum impact on your own effectiveness. The best way to cope with an abrasive personality is by refusing to become one.

GUILDELINES FOR RESOLVING AND AVOIDING CONFLICT SITUATIONS

◆ Make the effort to be an effective communicator. Conflicts are usually created because the parties involved don't understand each other's true meaning. Many of the recommendations in Chapter 10 will help prevent unnecessary conflicts by ensuring good communication.

◆ Replace defensiveness with openness. If you stop and think about it, all of the disruptive dozen are basically defensive personalities. People behave in these ways when they feel threatened. Consequently, the best way to discourage such behaviour is to behave in a non-threatening manner. The more you are receptive and open to the opinions and feelings of others, the less inclined they will be to go on the defensive.

On the other hand, if others perceive you as hostile or threatening, they will often withhold telling you bad news that you should know until it's too late. Remaining non-defensive and open to others' input can prevent minor problems from erupting into major catastrophes.

◆ When it is necessary to criticise the work or behaviour of others, do so kindly, helpfully and tactfully. If improperly handled, this can be another fertile ground for conflict. Here are five ideas for minimising conflict.

1. Choose the proper time and place, preferably somewhere private. Never publicly criticise or ridicule someone. You will only put them on the defensive, and defensive people don't listen.

2. Don't begin with the criticism. Start by paying the person a sincere compliment for something positive they have done. If you only criticise people, they will feel unappreciated and will likely be reluctant to pay attention to what you have to say.

3. Focus on the behaviour that needs correcting, not on the person. To the extent that you can indirectly call attention to the problem, do so. For example, you may have had a similar problem or made a similar mistake and may wish to discuss what you did.

4. Once you begin to discuss the problem, be specific. Telling Anna that her report is inadequate or Bill that he is doing a lousy job doesn't accomplish anything. If you want to help someone, point out specifically what needs to be corrected and recommend some possible alternatives.

5. End the discussion on a positive note. Express your willingness to help the person and your confidence that they can solve the problem if they want to.

For example, if you assigned an employee to gather information and write a report for you and the report isn't adequate, the gist of your message might be: 'Anna, you obviously spent a great deal of time and energy on this project and I sincerely appreciate what you've done. However, more data is needed in order to provide me with the information I need to make an intelligent decision. What I need is a greater emphasis on potential sales trends rather than dwelling on past data. I know our marketing research department has the necessary information to aid you in this task. Once you have combined this information with your talent for summarising and report writing, I am confident that this will be a first-rate document.'

◆ Before criticising someone else, make sure your own behaviour is in order. Remember that when we point a finger at someone else, four of our fingers are pointing back at us!

◆ Be assertive rather than aggressive. You can resolve conflicts and satisfy your own needs without dominating the other party or clubbing them into submission. Aggressive people are usually victims of the 'some gotta win, some gotta lose' myth. In most situations, it's possible to resolve conflicts and have everyone win to some degree.

Being assertive means expressing your feelings and satisfying your own needs in a pleasant and congenial manner. It means being responsible for your own feelings and assuming that others are responsible for theirs. Assertive people are open and honest about their feelings and feel free to confront others in a non-hostile way. It means saying yes when it is in your own best interests and no when it is not. And most of all, it means not allowing yourself to be intimidated by the aggressive behaviour of others.

◆ Mind your own business. Spreading hearsay about the business of others is ultimately never in your own best interests. In the course of our daily lives, a discussion about others is sure to arise and not all of it will be pleasant. Most gossip cannot be verified and is of no consequence anyway. By passing it along, you only brand yourself as party to the unsavoury business of rumour spreading, and such a practice can even get you sued for slander. As the American writer Mark Twain remarked, 'A lie can travel half way around the world while the truth is putting on its shoes.'

◆ Live and let live. It has been said that one person's rights end where another person's nose begins. Such a philosophy makes a great deal of sense when it comes to conflict. People's inability to tolerate and respect another's values or lifestyle is the cause of many conflicts, ranging from petty arguments to world wars.

Related to this is our neurotic need to find a scapegoat when things go wrong. Our laws have traditionally been based on some-one always being at fault, hence the guilty party in court cases. John had the right of way; therefore, the accident wasn't his fault. Karla proved that Hendrik deserted her; therefore, the failure of their marriage is Hendrik's fault.

This is not to say that we shouldn't be held responsible for our actions, for indeed we should. However, blaming is passing a moral judgement on others according to your own particular value system. You are in effect condemning them for not living up to your expec-tations, and such behaviour breeds hostility and frustration that is guaranteed to hurt only you. 'You can tell people to go to hell, but it's pretty hard to make them go.' Meanwhile, you waste your time moralising about this or that person, and the result is often more unnecessary conflict.

◆ Keep your cool. When you encounter a potential conflict situation, make delay your first strategy for avoiding it. For example, if some-one makes a statement that you find offensive, your best initial response is to ask the person what they mean. You may not have heard or understood them correctly. If you decide that you are being attacked, consider your alternatives. Is it really in your own best interests to retaliate in kind? Retaliation is usually just a waste of time. Very few things in life call for an instantaneous decision, particularly when you are working with others. To the extent that you think about situations before reacting to them, you will succeed in avoiding unnecessary skirmishes.

◆ Remember that arguing for the sake of arguing is a waste of time. Two people in verbal combat rarely achieve anything except loss of time, energy and, perhaps, their friendship.

If you want to convert someone to your way of thinking, arguing will only make the other person cling more tenaciously to their old position. You must first be willing to listen to them and try to understand their point of view before they will consider listening to yours. Assuming they are willing to listen, try to indirectly guide them towards discovering your point of view rather than taking an authoritarian 'that's the way it is' approach. As the French mathematician and theologian Blaise Pascal pointed out, 'People are usually more convinced by reasons they discovered themselves than by those found by others.'

◆ Don't rain on the other person's parade. We all have achievements and possessions that we point to with pride and that mean a great deal to us. Such things might be our home, our job, our education, our family, our car or our sporting trophies. Belittling or ridiculing someone else's achievements almost always generates conflict. Telling Stephen that you don't like the colour of the new car he just went into debt to acquire, or pointing out to Petra that the computer software she just bought has already been superseded are good ways to make enemies. To quote an anonymous source, 'A wise monkey never monkeys with another monkey's monkey.'

On the other hand, you will find people much more inclined to feel harmonious towards you if you make the effort to sincerely and openly compliment those things that they are proudest of. I'm not suggesting insincere flattery, but honest and specific recognition. Don't just tell Stephen that you like his new car. Tell him what you like — the colour, the style, the CD player, the vinyl top or whatever.

◆ Don't be a prophet of gloom and doom. Life is filled with people who believe that the world is going to hell in a basket. If you are inclined to be such a person, I would suggest that you make it easy on yourself by keeping your pessimistic opinions to yourself. To those of us who enjoy life, your gloomy presence is about as welcome as a decaying mackerel.

We don't want to hear about Jason's skiing accident or the latest plane crash when we are preparing to fly to the snowfields for a well-earned holiday. We understand the risks and are prepared to take them. It's unfortunate that Oliver's predecessor had to give up his job because it was too stressful. However, constantly reminding Oliver of this won't help him become any more effective. Therefore, as another antidote to unnecessary conflict, cheer up or shut up.

◆ If a major ongoing, unavoidable conflict is hindering your effectiveness, meet it head-on and discuss it with those involved. Sweeping conflicts under the rug only ensures that they will cause greater problems later on. Try to see the problem from the other person's perspective and they will likely reciprocate.

◆ Refuse to involve yourself in the games of the critic, moralist, martyr, trivia generator, cynic or anyone else who tries to waste your time and energy. It takes two people to play these games, so refuse to co-operate. If you want to be effective, you don't have the time or energy to devote to such counter-productive pastimes.

REMEMBER

Make the effort to be an effective communicator.

Work constructively, positively and responsibly with your colleagues.

The ability to delegate is one of the keys to success. Don't try and do everything yourself.

It is easier to work with people than it is to work against them.

Beware of the 12 problem people.

PART 5

LOOKING
AHEAD

CHAPTER 12

TAKING ADVANTAGE OF THE CHANGING WORK PLACE

*One must never lose time
in vainly regretting the past
nor in complaining about the changes
which cause us discomfort,
for change is the very essence of life.*
ANATOLE FRANCE

WE ARE LIVING at a special and exciting time. A time in which changes are taking place on an unprecedented scale. The work place is changing. Improvements in technology and the ever increasing power of the information super highway are impacting on countries, markets, industries and businesses, as well as on you and me.

The re-engineering revolution is changing the face of management structures in organisations all over the world. Executive power is being redefined and top managers no longer own the big picture. The rise of the Internet, indeed the whole communications boom, is having its effects on traditional job security. Jobs are being redefined and many are disappearing. Your job is no longer guaranteed, but the good news is that there will always be plenty of work. So, try changing your focus and you will discover that you have a whole new range of opportunities open to you. As one who made this shift from 'job' to 'work' some years ago, and who has absolute confidence in a profitable and pleasurable future, let me encourage you to embrace the new order with confidence and enthusiasm. So, ask yourself the following questions and go for it!

---◆---

How can I find my way through the confusion and chaos created by this massive change?

What will the changes mean to me and my family?

What must I do to prepare myself to be an effective and productive part of this new society?

What strategies do I need to implement to ensure that I make the most of the opportunities that are emerging as a result of these changes?

---◆ — ◆ — ◆---

While the task is daunting, the challenge is exciting and full of the promise of a future more rewarding than we can imagine. It is part of humanity's evolutionary process to face change, conquer it and move on. We have always been at our best during times of great change and challenge, and this time should be no exception. Throughout history, there have always been winners as well as losers. The challenge for each of us is to be among those who win and move on to fresh challenges, and we can make certain of that result by being prepared.

SEEING NEW OPPORTUNITIES

The first step in taking advantage of opportunities is to be actively looking for them. Once you have identified an opportunity, you must then be willing to act. The opportunity you have and don't take will be no more profitable than the opportunity you didn't have and couldn't take.

The next step is to learn to see the world with new eyes. We are all restricted by our own particular paradigms. We filter incoming data through these paradigms and, as a result, we see very clearly what we usually see and expect to see. When something new or unexpected comes along, we often fail to see it or choose to ignore it. Thus, we tend to see what we want to see, hear what we want to hear and believe to be true what we want to be true. In doing so, we expect tomorrow to be like today. We try to solve today's problems with yesterday's solutions, and we seek the future by looking through yesterday's eyes.

It is not easy to break the habits of the past. It requires persistence and discipline, but it is essential if we are to be successful in this new and different society that is being created. I suggest that you read everything you can find on paradigms. Books such as Joel Barker's *Future Edge* explain why we don't see many opportunities until someone else has already taken advantage of them.

A good example of a paradigm is the Swiss watch industry. In 1967 the Swiss dominated the world watch market, with over 50 per cent of the market by volume and around 80 per cent in terms of dollar turnover. Yet, three years later, the Swiss watch industry accounted for less than 20 per cent of the market's volume and dollar value.

How could this happen? How could a country that had dominated an industry to such an extent suddenly lose its way? It happened because of a paradigm shift in the industry. The cause was the quartz watch: totally electronic, no moving parts and highly accurate. The Swiss watch of the day couldn't compete.

As a market leader, why couldn't they have seen the emergence of this new product? Like their competitors, they monitored new inventions and kept a close eye on the market in terms of innovations. In fact, the Swizz themselves had invented the quartz watch. But when their research and development people showed them this new invention, they rejected it as having no real future in the industry. Why? Because they saw it through their old watchmaker's paradigm. It was too different from the watch of the day, so they rejected it. When, soon after, the prototype was exhibited at the World Congress of Watch Manufacturers, Seiko of Japan and Texas Instruments of the United States saw it and the Swiss lost an industry. So confident were the Swiss in their decision not to develop the quartz watch, they didn't even patent it. Who dominates the world watch market today? Japan.

An understanding of paradigms is critical to your future, for two reasons. First, you will be faced with an ever-increasing rate of change for the rest of your life. Unless you can see the world with new eyes, you may miss your chance. Second, if you are to perform a positive role in the future, you will need to become your own futurist. You will need to be able to anticipate the future to a degree where the decisions you make will be right more often than wrong. Unless you develop this skill, you will forever be playing catch up, and that puts you in the role of follower. There is nothing wrong with being a follower, as long as you are a good one. A good follower is one who is well-informed and focused on the common good.

In life, our choices seem to be either:

◆ Be as great a leader as you can; or
◆ Be as great a follower as you can.

But don't become someone who won't lead *or* follow and who just keeps causing problems for others. In the past, job security and full employment offered a middle ground where it wasn't always necessary to give one's best. Today, it's lead well, follow well or perish.

If we are to be a player in the new working environment, we must constantly search for new knowledge. One way of doing this is through networking, which provides an expanding source of information and opinions. As Peter Drucker says, 'opinions are the critical issue' and the better your source and quality of opinions, the better your chances of turning collective opinions into positive, effective results.

Networking is like gardening. It is a constant activity of sowing, tending and reaping, and the more effectively you tend your networking garden the more it will flourish. Giving to others is what makes it possible to receive from others. The more you give, the more you receive. The world as we know it today will change to such an extent and so quickly that it will be impossible to become expert in every facet of what we need to know to play an effective part. Knowing others who can provide expertise as and when required will be critical to our success.

Now let's explore some ways in which we can take advantage of opportunities in the following critical areas:

- new organisational structures
- the power of the individual
- the power of the customer
- jobs versus work.

NEW ORGANISATIONAL STRUCTURES

All organisations must grow or die, because the only way to coast is downhill. The difference in the future will be in the way they grow in organisational terms. In many ways, the modern organisation is moving towards a franchise-style structure. A management body will assist many small, independently managed busines units that share the same core principles and aims. However, each business unit still maintains day-to-day control over how they adapt their business to meet local conditions and the needs of their customers. The concept of starting out at the bottom of an organisation and working our way up through the ranks to the top will largely disappear. Middle management levels, which were largely channels for the dissemination of information, are being eliminated as speedier communications make them redundant.

The goal of several of the world's largest and most effective organisations is ultimately to have no more than three levels of management. While this may seem a drastic measure, competition will drive most organisations to adopt these standards. The elimination of management levels is not simply an exercise in cost cutting.

- It enables swifter and more effective communication.
- It puts the decision making process closer to the customer.
- It provides greater flexibility, so that senior management can adapt quickly to the changing business environment.

The move towards self-directed work teams arranged around specific skills and resources is seen by many organisations as the preferred way of achieving these results. The characteristics of these teams are:

- The team is made up of a number of workers who have a diversity of skills. It is focused entirely on results.
- The team is responsible for its own day-to-day management. The team decides for itself how, when and under what conditions it will function.

- Usually, current managers or supervisors become team leaders and exert minimal supervision over the team.

- Team members are empowered to take control of their jobs and, as a result, they are work-driven rather than management-driven.

- The team is given the resources, information, authority and responsibility necessary for it to become truly self-directed.

Teams succeed because the workers are empowered, they share information equally, and all members of the team take part in group decisions. Teams have authority to make decisions and responsibility for their results. All the team members learn leadership techniques, which raises motivation levels.

Some of the challenges that teams have to meet, and some reasons why they fail, are:

- The concept of the team challenges many people's ideas about how to control and run a business.

- Not everyone wants to be empowered. There are many people within organisations who are quite happy to do what they are told and who avoid having to make decisions. They don't want the authority or the responsibility that goes with being a team member. As a result, they find the team structure unappealing or even threatening.

- Some people might suspect that the power given to the team is a management plot against organised labour.

- Some people simply prefer to stick to the old ways, and find the prospect of the unknown a threat.

The existing hierarchical system will still be necessary for some organisations, though to be successful they will need to embrace the principles and practices of teams even though they don't have a team structure.

The principles of self-directed teams will apply to every position. And every person will need to be trained in management techniques. The old idea that only managers should be trained in management techniques has no place in the organisation of the future.

How can we ensure that we are ready to share in the opportunities presented by these new organisational structures?

Personal strategy

- Read all you can on why the structure of organisations is changing. Attend seminars on the subject and discuss your views with others whose opinions and performance you respect.

- Identify organisations that are in the process of change and contact people within those organisations who can explain the reasons for the changes. This will give you a broad understanding of what is happening in the market place.

- Cultivate a team outlook which takes account of all members' views.

- Be flexible in your thinking and search for a variety of solutions to perceived problems.

- Be assertive, not aggressive, in putting your views to the team.

- Accept that not all of your ideas and views will be accepted by the team. Being a poor loser will only create resentment, whereas acceptance of others' views will earn you respect and trust. Those who listen to others find that they are listened to more often and more openly.

- Be innovative and creative. Read *Innovation and Entrepreneurship* by Peter Drucker.

- Most teams will be staffed by people with different skills, and each member will be expected to be a top performer in their field of expertise. Ensure that you keep up to date in every area of your particular field.

- Be willing to accept responsibility and authority. Become work-driven and focus always on results.

- Learn as much as you can about management principles and practices. If you aspire to team leadership, then develop people management skills. Read Peter Drucker's *The Effective Executive*.

- Develop a can-do and will-do attitude. Believe and act as if everything is possible. If you are positive in your attitude and encourage others to be the same, you will gain credibility as a positive, results-oriented person.

- Develop your own long-term outlook on why these new organisational structures will work and how you can help to implement and maintain them.

- Understand that change will be continuous and that adapting will be a constant challenge for everyone. If you can be a leader in implementing changes and be constantly on the look-out for the next innovation, you will stand out in the organisation and increase your chances of profiting from the changes.

THE POWER OF THE INDIVIDUAL

When the first earth satellite was launched by the Russians in 1957, the information society forecast by Peter Drucker some 40 years ago was born. Today, around 60 per cent of workers in modern technology-based societies are information workers, and their main tool is the computer. Technology is changing the way we market, the way we communicate and the way we work. Today, information is the product. And the winners are those who can provide it and turn their knowledge into effective results.

The information revolution has placed the individual at the centre of all the changes that are taking place. John Naisbitt and Patricia Aburdene said in their book *Megatrends 2000*, 'The great unifying theme at the conclusion of the 20th century is the triumph of the individual.' This change to recognising the individual is affecting every aspect of work within every type of organisation.

Intellectual capital and intellectual capacity are being acknowledged by organisations as their chief asset. When management talk about intellectual capital, they are talking about you and me. As an individual, you are an important part of the company you work for. Money, buildings, machinery and other *assets* don't think. Only people can solve problems and work together to create, design, recruit, teach, motivate and inspire.

Without people, a business is only organised rubble. Indeed, the successful businesses now, and of the future, will be those that acknowledge and invest in their intellectual capital. But these intellectual resources are highly mobile. No one can own them except the individuals themselves. Intellectual capacity provides us with our right to work and is our passport to financial freedom.

For managers steeped in authoritarian traditions, this growth and recognition of the power of the individual in the work place will be a problem unless they are willing to radically alter their old attitudes. How to treat people so that they are encouraged to perform to their capacity will become the big issue. A major requirement will be the development of trust. Mutual trust can be the glue that binds the individual and the organisation together.

As individuals, we need to focus on improving our intellectual capacity so that we are assured of an effective role in the working environment of the future. Those who accept the challenge will survive and prosper, while those who procrastinate and try to get by on yesterday's skills and knowledge will slowly sift to the bottom of the heap. The whole thrust of modern society is making it more necessary than ever to work smarter, not harder.

Business is already reflecting this shift from process to outcomes and results. Here are some ways to turn what we know into effective results.

Personal strategy

◆ Focus on your own intellectual capacity and stretch yourself to reach your true potential in this vital area. The one certainty of our present capacity is that its usefulness to our present and future employers will decrease rapidly unless we follow a self-development program and stay ahead of the changing market place.

◆ The blocks to achieving our true potential as an individual are the same as those that inhibit organisations. We see ourselves as we are today and project our future based on who we are now, rather than on who or what we could become. We need to reinvent ourselves by removing these blocks. One way of doing this is by asking ourselves such questions as: 'What would I need to do to double my income?' 'What can I do to dramatically increase my personal potential?' 'What is my personal strategy?' 'How might I market myself?' 'On a scale of 1 to 5, how do I rate in my area of expertise?' 'Am I matching my potential to the key issues I see emerging in the market place?'

◆ Ask yourself 'what if' questions. 'What if I changed my distribution, doubled my sales force, adopted self-directed teams, focused my entire organisation on the customer, went into direct mail, started a frequent buyer club, or formed strategic alliances with other creative organisations to use some of their unused potential in terms of distribution, sales, marketing and advertising?'

◆ Do you have unused capacity in designing, packaging, sales or marketing? Do you have a component or a procedure that you could sell as a product or service that has the potential to create a business-within-a-business? Out-sourcing is a popular option today; what about in-sourcing? There are opportunities everywhere if we can put the past behind us and look to the future.

◆ Look at some of the present trends to see if they exploit our full potential. Does bench marking or best practice, for instance, inspire us to reach our full potential, or does it fixate us on someone else's past achievements? Does the methodology of the system bury us in detail, or does it fire our imagination, stir our creativity and encourage us to be innovative? Imagination, creativity and innovation are the stuff of reaching our true potential. They don't appear on the balance sheet, but without them the bottom line will not reflect the true potential of the business.

THE POWER OF THE CUSTOMER

The customer now rules the market place. Yet, the reality in many organisations is that the customer still comes a long way down the priority list. They might attend to the cosmetics of customer service by setting up a department specifically to deal with customer queries and complaints, and staff might be instructed to smile and be helpful to customers. As long as the customer behaves predictably and makes no demands outside the normal activities of the business, there aren't too many problems. However, there aren't many pluses either. An organisation that is satisfied with the *status quo* and doesn't actively pursue an aggressive policy of creating services and opportunities for customers is limiting its potential.

The critical issue for all organisations today is differentiation — how to make itself different in the perception of the customer, because it is that difference that draws the customer. Unique products and services are hard to come by; so the more products or services we sell that can be obtained from other sources, the more important differentiation becomes. The difference that the customer perceives, is their reason for doing business with an organisation.

Today, any business that does not have the customer as its first priority is trading on borrowed time. If it is not reorganising, downsizing or making other changes in order to serve the customer better, then its customers will go elsewhere.

The power of the customer is changing the way businesses sell their products and services, as well as the nature of those products and services. The customer has changed the way businesses compete. Customers are the reason a business exists and its only source of profits.

Anyone who wants to succeed in today's customer-driven market place will need to become an advocate for the customer. Here is how you can profit from new opportunities in this field.

Personal strategy

◆ Read everything you can about customers and consumer behaviour. If you understand how to win and keep customers, you will be able to play an important role in any organisation.

◆ Develop your understanding of customer satisfaction so that your concept embraces every part of the organisation as being responsible for their part in achieving customer satisfaction. If staff don't understand the specific role they should play in delivering total satisfaction, find out why. The front line is responsible for interacting with the customer, but they don't decide policy or develop new products, write advertising or decide pricing strategies, and they have nothing to do with board decisions that impact on customers. The problems don't lie with the front line; they stem from the people who make the decisions.

◆ Talk to people who run their own businesses. Ask them what they themselves value in terms of customer service and satisfaction, and how well their needs are being satisfied by their suppliers.

◆ Attend customer service seminars and develop strategies for delivering world-class customer service and satisfaction.

◆ Evaluate the customer service ethic in your organisation in terms of world standards.

JOBS VERSUS WORK

We hear constantly in the media about the job losses caused by technological advances. The days of jobs for everyone are over. Jobs are being eliminated because as a function of work they no longer fit the work patterns of the future. Jobs are too structured for the new and increasingly flexible organisation that is the business of the future.

What we will have in the future is work, not jobs. And the good news is that there will be plenty of work for those who want to do it. (I gave up jobs some years ago and have never been busier in my work.) The work we do may be different from what we have been used to. It will certainly be structured differently: more team-oriented, more flexible, more short term and almost totally results-oriented. In other words, we are moving back to how we used to work before jobs were invented.

As technology advances, it will provide work in plenty; the problem is our emotional attachment to the security of jobs. Some people will find the loss of the financial and structural certainty of jobs traumatic. And if they continue to chase jobs instead of looking for work, they may experience difficulty in adjusting to the new working environment because their focus is on the past instead of the future. But for others who can look to the future with new eyes and see work that needs to be done and are able to sell themselves as the person to do it, the changing work place will prove a bonanza. It's a simple matter of working smarter, not harder.

Your age and occupation, and whether you currently have a job with a long-term future or your present job is under threat, will affect how you should respond to the current trends.

Personal strategy

◆ If your current job has long-term possibilities, you should accept that it will change in the manner I have outlined. You should therefore prepare yourself in every way possible to play an active and important role in the transition of your organisation from what it is today to what it must become if it is to be successful tomorrow. Use the methods described in this chapter. Be a leader.

◆ If your current job is in jeopardy, decide now whether you want to try and stay in it. If you do wish to keep it, then work out how you can play a part in helping your organisation to move forward. Once you have decided what role you could play, sell the idea to the appropriate person. If you decide, instead, to leave, then remember it is not the end; it is more likely to be the start of a more profitable and happy future for you.

◆ If you are currently not employed, decide whether you will continue to look for a job or join those of us who look for work.

Your decision will probably depend on your age, type of occupation and experience. If you are just starting out, it is probable that you will look for a job. But remember that any job you get will be subject to the types of changes that have been outlined in this chapter, and that these changes will occur sooner than you might expect. Waste no time in understanding the full implications of these changes and accept that they will affect you. The only question is when.

- If you are further along in the journey of life, then you should accept the changes as having already affected your life and prepare for a new and different future. This future will possibly mean working for yourself, and what a wonderful future it can be. Think of all the things you said you would do if you were in charge; well, now you are, so do them. Take charge of your life. Consider the range of work you can do, and then focus on what you most like doing. Decide who could use this work and in what way they could use it. Draw up a strategy for selling your talents to those who can benefit from using them, and then go out and sell them your ideas.

- Read all you can about being self-employed. Subscribe to magazines on the subject and attend seminars on how to run a small business.

- Depending on the type of business you want to focus on, explore the possibilities of a franchise. This will provide you with background management support but day-to-day independence.

- If you decide to become a consultant in your area of expertise, develop your networking skills and seek advice from others already in the consulting business.

CONCLUSION

The power of the individual might seem to be a contradiction in terms to anyone who is feeling confused or threatened by the changes taking place in their work environment. Everywhere there is evidence that the individual is under a great deal of stress. The comfortable, dependable life we had only a few years ago has disappeared, and in its place we are confronted daily with a barrage of new challenges. The certainty we had in our lives that made it possible to plan for the long term and to watch our plans unfold has gone forever. We worry about our children, whose expectations have had to change. Some young people are giving up before they even start. The bad news of the day fills the media until we start to feel we have lost our way. Yet there are millions of people who are facing the challenges with courage and confidence and who have an unwavering belief in a prosperous and happy future for themselves and their families.

How easy will it be for you to take advantage of the new opportunities in the work place? Remember that this is the age of the individual. It is the greatest time in the history of humanity for the individual to flourish and prosper. It is time for each of us to assert our right to the future we long to have. But if we accept that it is the age of the individual, then we must also accept that the responsibility for making it happen in our lives lies with us.

Here is more good news. We have the power of choice. So choose wisely. Choose success, not failure. Choose happiness, not sadness. And choose wealth, not poverty. Above all, choose to be your own futurist. Grab these opportunities with both hands and head into the future with confidence. You live in an expanding universe in a time of expanding opportunities, so expand your vision to see the big picture and go after your place in it. And you can best do that by working smarter, not harder.

CHAPTER 13

SUMMING UP—
DO YOU NOW WORK SMARTER, NOT HARDER?

*Queer thing, but we think
every other man's job
is easier than our own.
And the better he does it,
the easier it looks.*
EDEN PHILLPOTTS

THE PURPOSE OF this book has been to give you some simple, practical techniques for making the most of your time and energy. Those who work smart are not loafers looking for the easy way out. Rather, they are people who make the most of their lives and thus create greater personal satisfaction for themselves and those they come in contact with. They are effective people.

These individuals don't necessarily possess abilities that set them apart from the rest of us. They simply realise that by applying a few powerful ideas, they can have an easier, more satisfying and productive life. In this chapter, I would like to summarise some of the main ways to increase your effectiveness. Much of this review is in the form of a series of questions. I hope you will refer frequently to this chapter, especially if you find your effectiveness is less than satisfactory.

◆ Do you focus on results? Effective people know it's more important to do the right job than to do the job right.

◆ Are you willing to invest the work to get what you want out of life? Sometimes effectiveness means investing time and effort in projects whose rewards are in the distant future. However, effective people never underestimate the importance of enjoying today. While they are future-oriented, they also have the common sense to realise that there is no inherent incompatibility between enjoying today and building for a better tomorrow. The two ideas are viewed as complementary.

◆ Have you identified any work tapes you may be playing? Much of what we were taught about work is only partially true, at best. Someone who is successful may tell you how hard they have worked. But sweat, activity, efficiency, hours and pressure are not linked to accomplishment in a predictable fashion. Every job is unique and requires different combinations of blood, sweat, tears, time and intelligence in order to be successfully completed. Remember that effectiveness is more of an art than a science, and constantly practise refining your skills.

◆ Have you set your own goals and accepted total responsibility for achieving them? Goals are necessary for your happiness, as well as being the vehicle that enables you to concentrate your time and energy most effectively. Set goals that are specific, challenging, realistic and measurable. Be sure your goals are compatible and give each one a deadline. Put your goals in writing, but consider them subject to revision and change.

When you set your goals, set them on a lifetime, intermediate and daily basis. After setting goals, rank them in order of importance and tackle the top-priority projects first. Remember the 80/20 rule. Eighty per cent of your effectiveness comes from achieving 20 per cent of your goals.

◆ Do you try to solve problems in a simple, rational way? Effective people appear to live a carefree, charmed existence when in fact they, like everyone else, encounter their share of life's problems. The difference between these people and others is that effective people realise that the number and severity of problems they have aren't as important as the way in which they are handled. They realise that becoming emotionally involved in a problem only lessens the chances of finding a satisfactory solution.

◆ Do you distinguish between urgent problems and important ones? The tyranny of the urgent can wreck your effectiveness if it is allowed to reign unchecked. Remember, urgent things are seldom important and important things are seldom urgent.

◆ Have you accounted for your use of time? Most time use is habit and we don't know how we spend our time until we try to keep track of it. Keeping a time log periodically can help us to uncover and eliminate unproductive habits.

◆ Do you keep a loose schedule? A good rule of thumb is never to schedule more than 50 per cent of your day. Murphy's Law can play havoc with tight schedules. Expect the unexpected.

Schedule the most important tasks for prime time — the time of day when you work your best. Also set aside a period of time each day for reflecting on who you are and what your goals are. Look for ways to make multiple use of time that has already been committed.

◆ Do you know what not to do? Effectiveness doesn't result from doing more; it's the product of doing less better. The inability to say no is a great effectiveness killer. When you find it necessary to say no, do it promptly and politely to avoid raising unnecessary expectations. Don't feel you have to have a reason every time you refuse someone's request, but provide one if you deem it appropriate.

◆ Before tackling a job, do you ask yourself, 'Is this the best use of my time and energy?' If the answer is yes, equip yourself with the proper tools and complete the task. If the answer is no, get someone else to do the job or don't do it.

◆ Are you a workaholic? Accept the fact that time away from the job is a necessary stimulus to greater creativity, satisfaction and effectiveness on the job.

◆ Do you have a sound self-image? Do you know who you are? Recognise and accept your limitations and build on your strengths. You're better than you think.

Accept yourself unconditionally. It's the key to peace of mind, and a peaceful mind is a more effective one.

The majority of people strive to improve their image in the eyes of others, but the effective individual realises that other-directedness isn't nearly as important as inner-directedness. The very essence of an effective person is doing things that make them feel good about themselves.

◆ Do you put your own needs first? You can't help the poor by becoming one of them. Effective people are positively selfish. They refuse to be martyrs or self-sacrificers and give of themselves only when they have something meaningful to give. As a result, their help tends to be more abundant, effective and oriented towards helping others to help themselves.

◆ Do you accept responsibility for your own feelings? Do you believe that you, like everyone else, make your own sunshine? Have you said goodbye to the time- and energy-robbing emotions of guilt and worry? When you feel anger, have you learned to use it positively to move you towards your goals?

An antidote to excessive anger is a well-developed sense of humour. Take your work seriously, but not yourself. When things get hectic, back off, look at things in perspective and learn to laugh at yourself. Ninety-nine per cent of the time, things seem more important in the present than they actually are.

◆ Do you build on your strengths? If you perform work that allows you to build on your strengths, you will perform with relative ease. Take a relaxed approach towards your work. Remember that how well you work is far more important than how hard you work.

◆ Are you aware that being a perfectionist can cripple effectiveness? Somerset Maugham wrote, 'Only a mediocre person is always at his best.' Striving for perfection usually costs us more time than the increased benefits justify. Sometimes perfection is essential, and on those occasions, you should do your best to deliver it. However, most of the time it isn't necessary and wastes time that could be better spent doing something else.

◆ Do you have the courage to act and commit yourself to calculated risk-taking? The courage to take calculated risks is essential. The only other alternative is a wasted life of inaction, immobilisation and servitude to your fears. It's better to feel sorry for the things you've done than to waste your life regretting missed opportunities.

Our culture is very security-oriented, and caution is the norm.

However, to make the most of your life you must accept the fact that the only real security is that which comes from within. Despite what you have been told by your parents, teachers, spouse, clergy, employer or insurance companies, no one ever gives anyone security. Life is a gamble from the cradle to the grave, and refusing to take risks makes for a life of mediocrity.

Measure success in terms of what you gain and not what you lose. You will have your share of adversities, but these are experiences to learn from and not final acts. Mike Todd, the American showman, once remarked, 'I've been broke many times, but I've never been poor.' Eighty per cent of achievement is having the guts to try.

◆ Have you bid farewell to procrastination? Most of us are procrastinators to some degree. The important thing is to recognise it as a useless burden that must be minimised if you want to get things done with less effort.

◆ Are you a frequent and skilful delegator? Smart workers aren't plagued by do-it-yourselfitis. They concentrate on performing the important tasks that only they can do. Anything that can be delegated is delegated.

Realise that there are many irrational temptations to avoid delegating, and work to overcome them. Accept the fact that others will make mistakes and do the job differently. Work at developing your delegating skills. It's quite an art.

◆ Is your assistant given responsible, challenging assignments in addition to routine tasks? An intelligent, competent assistant is a priceless aid to effectiveness. Get a good one and seek to develop their potential. Many successful executives attribute much of their rise in fortune to the aid of competent and loyal assistants who helped them to climb the ladder of success. Keep them informed and reward their effectiveness with the support, salary and recognition they deserve.

◆ Do you make a conscious effort to improve your ability to communicate? The spoken, printed or written word may be woefully inadequate, but it is all that we have. Keep in mind that all communication is a symbolic process that is interwoven with our thought processes. We tend to start out speaking as we think, but end up thinking as we speak.

When communicating with others, look for total meaning and be aware of the common types of communication breakdowns. Consider the source as much as the message. If you don't understand someone, don't be embarrassed to ask questions. Communicate your thoughts in specific, simple, everyday language.

◆ Do you attempt to work with people rather than against them? Bertrand Russell once said, 'The only thing that will redeem mankind is cooperation.' Some conflicts are necessary, but most are a needless waste of time caused by poor communication.

Effective people resolve conflicts in a friendly, non-threatening manner. They are slow to criticise others, and remain cool and unthreatened in the face of criticism. Their inner security and ability to focus on the important things in life provide them with the ability to avoid, resolve or tolerate conflict.

Smart workers make life pleasant for themselves and those around them. They are perennial optimists in both work and deed. Because they like themselves, they find it easy to tolerate, accept and love the world and those around them.

◆ Have you taken steps to minimise interruptions? Meetings, visitors and telephone calls can derail our best-laid plans if we allow them to.

Avoid meetings like the plague. Don't be a habitual joiner. If it is necessary to call a meeting, have a specific purpose and agenda. Time spent planning meetings and focusing on goals during the meeting can greatly reduce their time and cost.

Shield yourself from drop-in visitors. Schedule visiting hours and see drop-in visitors only in cases of emergency. Arrange appointments for necessary visitors and have others screened.

Use the telephone intelligently to save time rather than waste it. Know who your frequent callers are. Receive and make telephone calls at specified times. When you wish to work uninterrupted, have your calls taken by your assistant, an answering service, or a telephone answering machine.

Get yourself a hideaway for serious, lengthy periods of uninterrupted work. Choose a quiet spot and let your whereabouts be known only to a privileged few.

◆ Are you controlling and reducing your paper work or wallowing in it? Paper is here to stay, but you don't have to let it clutter your life and smother your goals. If in doubt, throw it out. Never ask for anything on paper unless it is absolutely necessary. If you pick up a piece of paper, throw it away or do something to move it on its way. Never write when a telephone call or face-to-face contact will suffice. Paper is money.

When you have to write something, express yourself clearly, simply and naturally. The key to being an effective reader is not to read faster but more selectively. Knowing what not to read is far more important than how rapidly you read.

◆ Do you enjoy your work? Above all, remember that life is not to be endured but to be enjoyed. A life of satisfaction and happiness is what we all seek. However, we must have the good sense to realise that happiness doesn't result from inaction but rather from creative absorption.

◆ Have you accepted the changes that are taking place in terms of organisation structures, and are you willing to become an expert on why and how they will change the work place? Are you now prepared to play your part in them?

◆ Are you willing to do what needs to be done to ensure that you keep your own intellectual capacity at a high level, so that you will be prepared at all times to take whatever opportunities arise in your area of work?

◆ Will self-directed work teams become an opportunity or a threat to you? Are you prepared to become a team leader if it becomes necessary? Have you already attended the courses and bought the books and done the study to ensure that you are prepared? If you have, congratulations — you're on your way to winning.

◆ Do you understand the issues of real customer satisfaction? Are you willing to tackle the issue in your work place? Remember that the payoff for those who can convert their organisation to world-class customer service and satisfaction is enormous.

◆ Do you understand the difference between jobs and work? Are you willing to take advantage of the opportunities that work, not jobs, presents? Have you considered the benefits that could flow to you if you were to change from doing a job to doing your own work?

◆ Has the power of the individual taken a special place in your thinking? Are you preparing to exploit this shift in power from organisations to the individual? Do you have a list of what you can do in your life to create opportunities for yourself and your family as a result of this move to the individual? Whatever you do, make sure that you don't underestimate the potential of this paradigm shift in power.

If you can answer yes to most of these questions, then you really know how to work smarter, not harder. If you answered no, then start again; it's never too late to improve your situation. Try again, and your persistence will pay off.

Effective people have an intelligent type of persistence. They realise that most of us waste our time and energy by abandoning our goals too soon. Once these people attach themselves to a dream, they hang on for the ride and enjoy every minute of it. The best way is to get committed to an idea or a dream that is important to you. Without commitment, you will remain in the land of dreams. Most people never realise their full potential because they are never really committed.

NOW TO COMMITMENT

How do you rate in this business of commitment? Let me ask you some questions.

◆ How long is it since you worked for days with absolute dedication in order to achieve a goal?

◆ How long is it since you have achieved a goal against great odds?

◆ How long is it since you did something at great personal inconvenience in order to achieve a goal to which you were committed?

There are no prizes for answering these questions. The important thing is that you understand that commitment is the key to achieving. It is the result and evidence of strong motivation. Once you are motivated sufficiently to become strongly and totally committed to an ideal, a vision, a dream or an objective, the chance of success is multiplied.

Commitment is important. It's the bond you have with yourself. It's your personal contract to get the job done. It's the difference between talking and acting. Commitment is the fire you light within that won't go out, whatever difficulties you encounter. It's the fire that can only be extinguished by the achievement of the goal to which you are committed. Commitment is everything. Without it we are, at best, lost souls. We wander the world seeking a place. We invent goals to which we are not committed. We dream dreams to which we have no commitment. We make plans to which we owe no allegiance, and invariably they languish through lack of commitment.

Those who are the world's winners are different. They really do march to a different drum. They are the ones who know the rules. They have a system, and they apply a method. They are committed. They dream as a basis for decision making. They decide. They plan as a basis for accomplishment. They make things happen.

How, then, can you do what they do? You can do it by first understanding the process. By understanding why you behave as you do. With understanding comes the possibility of motivation — with motivation comes desire, and with the desire comes commitment. From commitment comes action, and from action come results, rewards and further motivation. Then the cycle of achieving is complete. It becomes a way of life. It becomes the winner's way. But, sadly, not for all. Many people spend their time on the lowest rungs of life's ladder waiting, hoping, longing for the chance that often never comes because life is not like that. Good things in life don't happen by accident. They happen on purpose. They happen by plan. Winning is not an accident — winning is succeeding by design.

Life is a self-fulfilling prophecy; as you think, so shall it be. The challenge is to start, to get going, to become one of life's great achievers. To use your motivation. To get the want to and the can do. To work smarter, not harder.

HOW YOU CAN DO IT

Work Smarter, Not Harder isn't a fantasy, nor is it just a great title for a book! It is about achieving more with less effort, making every day count and simply enjoying your life. This book can mark the beginning of your new attitude to work — with better use of your time and energy, you will have a happier and more productive life. I wish you every success in unlocking your real potential.

Commitment, as I see it, is the key issue. It's the driving force that makes it possible to persevere until you have accomplished your goal. Yet it often seems to be the missing ingredient. Perhaps it has something to do with the hectic lifestyle we lead in the 1990s. Striking the balance between quality of life and setting and achieving goals is difficult — too often it seems that our goals take second place. It is not my purpose to tell you how you should run your life, but it is important to remember that desire without commitment is of little use. Commitment and persistence are a powerful pair. Thomas Edison, the father of electricity, failed in over 2000 experiments before he achieved his goal. Be committed to your dreams, your ideas, your goals! Go for it! WORK SMARTER, NOT HARDER.

REMEMBER

Working smarter, not harder works! Believe and trust in the methods outlined in this book.

Understand that you can't move away from who you are; you can only move towards who you want to be. So focus on what it is you want to do or want to be.

Make your goals your dominant thought, because day by day we achieve our dominant thought.

Write down your goals. Plan your lifetime and business goals.

- ◆ This is what I want.
- ◆ This is when I want it.
- ◆ This is how I will know when I have what I want.
- ◆ This is what I intend to give in return for what I expect to achieve.

Make a commitment not to rest until it is done. Nothing will be so tough or so difficult that it will prevent you from achieving your goal.

NOW do what needs to be done until your goals have been achieved. Then comes the pleasure of achievement and the satisfaction and rewards of accomplishment.

Also available from Jack Collis

The Great Sales Book

*Jack Collis is a legend in sales performance. He delivers
refreshing, practical and dynamic insights for successfully
operating in the competitive sales environment.*
BILL LEIGH, F.A.S.I

Not getting the sales figures you need to make budget?
Feel as though everyone is slamming the door in your face?
Running out of new and innovative ideas for presenting
yourself and your product? Don't despair! Jack Collis's
exciting new book, **The Great Sales Book** gives you all
the practical help and advice you need to maximise
your full selling potential.
The Great Sales Book offers useful, tried-and-tested
advice on how to increase your sales productivity. Benefit
from Jack Collis's years of experience as he guides you
through the psychology of selling, teaches you the art of
effective face-to-face communication and gives you
excellent tips on how to powerfully present yourself and
your product to get the results you want.

ISBN 0 7322 6634 3

Harper*Business*
An imprint of HarperCollins*Publishers*

YES YOU CAN

More timely advice and inspiration
from **Jack Collis**.

Do you feel as though your dreams are so far away
that you'll never get any closer
to what you want or to who you want to be?
If the answer is (with a deep sigh) 'yes',
then in the words of Peter Thorpe
(editor of Small Business & Investing),
Read this book. It could change your life.

Yes You Can is a guide to harnessing the power
of *your* mind to bring meaning, happiness and
prosperity into your life.

ISBN 0 7322 5818 9

Harper*Business*
An imprint of HarperCollins*Publishers*

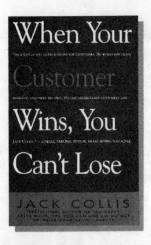

WHEN YOUR CUSTOMER WINS, YOU CAN'T LOSE

The rewards of customer loyalty are enormous.
The key to harnessing that loyalty is creating a service
which exceeds the customers expectations.

In this indispensable book, **Jack Collis** shows you how to:

- win customers more easily and more often
- generate and increase customer satisfaction
- keep customers coming back
- create strategies to increase staff effectiveness
- create a highly motivated team
- become more productive and profitable

Put simply, the difference between success and
failure can be the quality of your relationship
with your customers.

ISBN 0 7322 5911 8

Harper*Business*
An imprint of HarperCollins*Publishers*

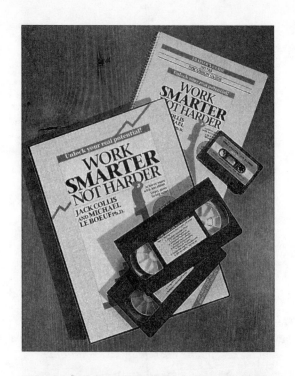

Work Smarter
Not Harder

Every minute counts, so why not get some more good advice from Jack and Michael . . .

On Video $345rrp

Video package includes:

- 2 x 25mins VHS video cassettes
- 1 x 25mins Trainer's guide audio cassette
- 1 x Trainer's guide booklet

On Audio $125rrp

Audio package includes:

- 6 audio cassettes x 50mins
- 1 x Trainer's guide booklet

Work
Smarter
Not
Harder